Living with Crossdressing

Defining a New Normal

*Observations and Thoughts for Non-Fetish,
Non-Transitioning Crossdressers and the
Women Who Love Them*

Written by Savannah Hauk

Library of Congress Control Number: 2017911736

ISBN 978-0-9914702-3-5
10 9 8 7 6 5 4 3 2 1

Covers by Savannah Hauk
Edited by J. Swain

The opinions expressed in this book are solely the thoughts
of those involved in its writing, and are in no way
meant to replace a professional's opinion or counsel.

Copyright 2017 by Savannah Hauk
All rights reserved.

LivingWithCrossdressing.com
Follow on Facebook @livingwithcrossdressing

Hoping that people of all faiths, ethnicity, gender, and orientation can come together in love and understanding – beyond simple tolerance.

Remember, tolerance can be defined as simply resisting the urge to prohibit the expression and ideas that we find unpleasant or disagreeable. Acceptance begins with embracing and celebrating those different than us.

Acknowledgements

I would like to thank everyone I have met on my crossdressing journey for this feminine creature who I call Savannah. They have provided an invaluable lifeline. You will get a sense of some of these people throughout this book.

First and foremost, I must thank the love of my life. Jen is a steadfast and free-spirited woman who has evolved with me as I have evolved. We complement each other. Our growing understanding of what the new normal could be is intriguing, exciting and all I could hope for.

I would like to thank my ex-wife for being part of my life when the move to New York City seemed insurmountable, otherwise. I wish her well in her own life's journey.

I'd like to wish to thank all of the couples that have so graciously accepted my invitation to share the intimate and sometimes painful details of their own journeys. They have enriched Jen and my life, just as I hope we have done for them. In their own subtle ways, they constitute a new forward-thinking tandem when it comes to what a relationship between a crossdressing man and a woman can be.

I would like to thank my closest friends who have shown Savannah their support. Love and hugs go out to my sister and her husband. Not every family member would be so open-minded.

This list also includes all of my Savannah gurlfriends (men who are transgender) who continue to raise me up, never questioning my passions.

Finally, I send out a thank you to all others who have touched my life in some way. One way or another, you have steered me to be the person you see before you.

Quick Notes

PRONOUNS

I understand that heated discussions rage around the concept of proper pronoun usage. I don't wish to offend any individual by using the wrong masculine or feminine pronoun to describe them. But for ease of reading and understanding for the novice – especially for those readers who are new to the community – I will be using the masculine pronouns of *he*, *him*, and *his* when referring to men and to crossdressing men. I will be using *she* and *her* when referring to cis-women. Transgender women will also be described as *gurls* or *gurlfriends*, where appropriate in the storytelling.

As the debates on gender identity and identification continues, and new gender qualifiers become more popular, I am sure my pronoun usage throughout this book will quickly become archaic and unusable. Please be as accepting of this book as you hope people will be accepting of you, as this book is written in one moment in time where the prevailing societal 'normal' is still that a man is he and a woman is she.

LABELS

There are many labels for the people who identify as crossdressers and transgender in the LGBTQ community. I have spoken to a few transitioned MtF women who have different opinions as to whether crossdressers should be considered part of the transgender community. In my writing, I will be taking the position that crossdressers are under the transgender umbrella in an effort to portray an inclusive and united community. I do mean to offend anyone's sensibilities as to their own interpretation of how they label others, only to bring us all together in a tighter bond of unity.

THE COMMUNITY

There are dozens of splinter groups within the LGBTQ community. From crossdressers to post-operative transsexuals, there is a vast spectrum of gender identities and sexual preferences. I do not mean to exclude anyone from my discussions, but I will be focusing primarily on crossdressing men and the cis-women who have chosen to stay partners with them. Just know that I have love and positivity for all of my brothers and sisters in the community in the hopes that they will have love and positivity for me in return.

Living with Crossdressing

Defining a New Normal

Observations and Thoughts for Non-Fetish, Non-Transitioning Crossdressers and the Women Who Love Them

Written by Savannah Hauk

Table of Contents

Am I Being Too Foreword?	13
History Of Crossdressing	17
You Might Be A Crossdresser If…	22
Why We Do It	48
Lifers And Late Bloomers	57
Truth And Consequences	65
Savannah's Story	71
Our Story – Savannah & Jen	91
Jen, In Her Own Words	111
The Last Crusade	120
Other Stories – A Fairytale	123
Other Stories - Crosses to Bear	134
Other Stories – Late To The Party	151
Other Stories – Amanda…	164
The New Gurl	176
Masculinity vs Femininity	181
Have You Heard That Joke?	199
From Closet To Coatrack	205
The Purge	212
What Is Normal?	215
Balancing Acts	220
Haters Hate	227
My Better Half	236
Sex, Lies & Videotape	249

Probing Questions	254
You Can't Handle The Truth	257
Reluctance	264
Is This Goodbye?	266
Resources & Bibiographies	269
Transgendered Terms	270
About The Author	281

Am I Being Too Foreword?

I do not possess a university degree in psychology, sociology or other sciences. I have at my disposal my observations and experiences with crossdressing. My credentials come from the School of Hard Knocks, as it were. I am a life-long crossdresser who has faced trials, self-doubt, and my share of worry about the known and fear of the unknown.

I have experienced shame, unhappiness and loneliness as a result of being viewed as ab*normal* by the general populace. But I have no shame for the man I am, for the woman I am… for the human being I am.

I finally decided to write down my thoughts and opinions on the subject of crossdressing, as a result of social media. That may seem like a strange notion… writing a book when I could be posting on my blog, vlog, YouTube channel or Twitter feeds like all the Millennial kids out there. I'm old school, simple as that. The anonymity that social media provides allows everyone to have an opinion (which they have a right to), but positive messages have gotten lost in the midst of the outpouring of intolerance and ignorance. I found my heart saddened to the point where I felt I must speak up.

Another reason, a more important reason, is that a man who needs to express himself as a woman faces solitude, shame and secrecy when in a relationship with a cis-gender woman (a cis-gender individual indentifies with their biological sex) because they have a fear of being rejected and misunderstood. Where is the support for these men and their partners? Besides expensive marriage and couples counselors, there seems to be vague online community support for crossdressers and their significant others that, at times, seems to be quiet or defunct.

Imagine that you are the wife or girlfriend of a male crossdresser, either by admission or discovery. Imagine that you need to understand more about the situation you find yourself in. There is plenty of literature and websites out there to sift through. What do you find? There seems to be an endless parade of pantyhose-loving, hairy, corseted fetishists. You can read online fantasy fiction or watch Japanese hentai anime that may send a spike of fear into your heart. There are countless stories of crossdressing men who resort to surgery to alter their gender to that of a woman. It seems that all crossdressers are gay. What is this world in which my partner is involved?

I am not here to tell you that the road is paved, even, and easy to travel upon. There are victims on both sides of the relationship, but each must come together to better understand the other's perspective. Each must learn to stop, listen and put themselves in their partner's shoes.

Well, that should be easy! The crossdresser wants to wear her shoes anyway!

That adage is misleading because even though we (the crossdressers) understand the physical component of wearing her shoes (for me, the higher the heel the better) we cannot immediately grasp what it is like for a woman to come to grips with learning that the man they love is also sometimes a woman.

Many crossdressers have had years to come to terms with who they are. Sometimes, they are still a work in progress. Who am I kidding? We're always a work in progress!

But, we crossdressers have to understand that, regardless of when our partner is told about or discovers our feminine side, we are bound by love to communicate with her, be honest with her (and with ourselves), and be sensitive to her needs.

Have I caught your attention? Have I struck a chord within you? If so, I invite you to continue reading. Please take this journey with me. I can guarantee that, as the words flow from my fingers to the cursor blinking on the screen, I will be discovering more about myself as well.

I am, by no means, an expert on all things transgender. There are things that I don't know about the community and about life, for that matter. I accept that I am ignorant of many truths. That understanding and acknowledging allows me the capacity to learn.

Welcome, dear crossdresser. I hope I can illuminate your thinking and reflection on questions you may be struggling with. And a special welcome to you, the crossdresser's dear partner. You are the most important person in a crossdresser's life. I hope there is something of value in these pages that offers you a measure of enlightenment and hope. At the very least, please know that every word is written purely from my heart.

With warmest regards and love,
Savannah Hauk

History Of Crossdressing

We owe a lot to Thomas Edison - if it wasn't for him, we'd be watching television by candlelight.

~ Milton Berle

It's hard to feel macho in makeup and a dress!

~ Milton Berle

Pop Quiz

This is your history lesson. There may be a quiz at the end.

Crossdressing is not a modern concept. Throughout history there are examples of it in many societies and cultures. Starting with the mythologies (Greek, Roman, Norse, Hindu, others), many examples exist of men masquerading as woman or being transformed into a female. The gods were known to come down from the heavens and take the guise of the opposite sex for the whim of spying or interacting with us mere mortals.

Many historical documents reference the concept of crossdressing, whether male-to-female or female-to-male. The Bible, for instance, in Deuteronomy 22:5, includes the following passage:

"A woman shall not wear a man's garment, nor shall a man put on a woman's cloak, for whoever does these things is an abomination to the LORD your God."

Apparently, I'm an abomination!

I should stop writing now and start repenting!

Hey, I'm not here to preach to you about the sinful nature of the act of crossdressing. That is a personal belief. I simply illustrate that the writers of the Bible felt a need to speak to it. Many believe that the passage simply refers to the fact that to don the clothes of the opposite sex is a deceit and falsehood when used to such ends.

Throughout history, it was more common to see a woman take the guise of a man. In the last several hundred years, the social station of women in many cultures was that of a secondary citizen. What better way to gain respect, popularity for your ideas, and acceptance in society than by taking on the persona of the men you were trying to impress? Many women have served in various armies around the world, including decorated Catalina de Erauso, Ann Mills, and Dorothy Lawrence. They were bold and seemingly fearless, as their military records illustrate.

At the same time, men who dressed as women were perceived as deceitful and as lowering their station. Charles Edward Stuart, in 1745, supposedly dressed as Flora MacDonald's maidservant to escape having to serve for the Battle of Culloden. Peking Opera singer Shi Pei Pu dressed as a woman to elicit information from a French diplomat during the Cultural Revolution. Even Jefferson Davis of the Confederacy of the United States of America was rumored to have dressed as a woman to escape the pursuing armies of the Union.

To summarize, a woman dressing as a man was to be applauded. They masqueraded as men in order to elevate or gain stature or influence. On the other hand, a man dressing as a woman was to be looked on as demeaning, as they did so under the guise of fraud and deceit, and of negating their gender superiority.

Interesting.

In the modern era – the 20th and 21st centuries –women donning male-centric attire seems to hold little taboo (unless, of course, that woman portrays herself consistently in a very masculine manner). Women who simply prefer to wear jeans instead of skirts and dresses could all be considered crossdressers; bur the practice has become accepted as normal. For men, it has become more mainstream to take better care of their bodies (a la labeled a metrosexual).

In both instances, labels are still attached in order to make the acts better understood. Slap a label and a simple description on it, and people tend to grasp it a bit better. But neither of these examples has the stigma that the male crossdresser still encounters.

Throughout the ages, people have had a love affair with crossdressing in the entertainment industry. In the Far East (Kabuki) and Europe (Shakespeare), theater has enjoyed the portrayal of female characters by men. Some of this was due to the segregation of the sexes, but it does prove that there was an acceptance that men could dress as woman for theater.

This idea continued into the modern era. Milton Berle, Flip Wilson, and Benny Hill made careers out of parading around their stages as female characters. Jack Lemmon and Tony Curtis used their feminine wiles in *Some Like It Hot* to hide from the mob, getting into hilarious misadventures with Marilyn Monroe. That was in 1959.

Were these men considered crossdressers? Not typically. As far as we know these performers did not take the art of crossdressing further than the hot spotlights in front of their audiences. They entertained us for laughs. Parody, not personal expression, drove these characters. As an audience, we can appreciate the performance of the character and the context of the story. I am fairly certain that their portrayals did not cast them into the category of crossdressers. From Danny Boyle to Dustin Hoffman, from Patrick Swayze to Tom Hanks, each was not saddled with the stigma of being a transgender minority male. Even conservative leaning Rudy Guiliani dressed as a woman for a cameo Broadway role.

But cast that character in real life as someone you love and you will not necessarily be as happy or as entertained. Sitcoms last 22 minutes, movies last 2 hours. Partnerships are supposed to last a lifetime.

Two Trains Leave The Station At...

Seriously, you might be thinking, *that wasn't a very good history lesson.* And you would be right. I had not intended to bore you with statistics, dates and personal profiles. No one ever memorizes all of those things (unless you have 3" x 5" index cards). I simply wanted to give you a taste that crossdressing has been around for a long time.

Women have masqueraded as men in order to affect change or live grander lives. Most have been exulted for their courage and valor. Men across the ages, from the 1400s to the late 1800s, have singularly hoarded all of the fineries of satins, silks and powdered wigs. Those aristocrats were looked up to and envied for their fashion and status (of wealth and station). Heck, even Greek and Roman men and women wore robes, and it wasn't even a college frat party.

As with almost all species and cultures, males and females dress to impress and to show off their attributes. It's all about defining what will enhance the attraction of another. As our society has matured and become more accepting of the blurring of fashion lines, women in western culture have been embraced for wearing masculine fashions. Men can be conscious and take more meticulous care of their bodies (being accepted in some more suburban and metropolitan areas). It is the crossdressing male that continues to suffer as a result of his quest for a more complete feminine expression.

Why do men want to express themselves as women, or in some obvious feminine way, if they are not considering a transition into womanhood or are not gay? Continue our journey, dear reader, and let's see if together we can discover more about what motivates the male crossdresser.

You Might Be A Crossdresser If...

I believe that we are here for each other, not against each other. Everything comes from an understanding that you are a gift in my life - whoever you are, whatever our differences.

~ John Denver

If you own a home with wheels on it and several cars without, you just might be a redneck.

~ Jeff Foxworthy

Spectrum

There is a vast spectrum of behaviors and personalities that are defined under the umbrella of crossdressing. Each person is driven by his (or her) own slant of what they are striving to emulate, feel, or experience. There rage huge debates – from society in general to the ostracism from our own Lesbian, Gay, Bisexual, Transsexual, Questioning (LGBTQ) community – as to where crossdressers should be classified; as well as whether we are simply a fetish group that serves to destabilize and debase the "more serious" transgender factions.

What follows is a small cross-section of crossdressing stereotypes. This is by no means a complete list. Many crossdressers may have occupied more than one type (or occupy more than one type at the same time) during their lives. I'll never understand the fascination of some of the types you will read about, nor will I ever find common ground to agree with these crossdressing men's reasons or motivations. My job is not to judge but to set the table and let you pick at what you would like to consume.

Avid Readers

> *I felt faint.*
> *My freshly shaved skin tingled with the thought of wearing the lingerie that my wife had placed on the bed for me. The bra, panties, garters and stockings would look fantastic on any woman's figure...*

Many love to escape to a make-believe world of femme fantasy fiction. There are many fan sites dedicated to fictional feminization. They cover all types of fetish writing topics, including forced feminization, caught with consequences, bad boy to good girl, mind control, and more. In fact, some writers are so prolific that they have created an entire fictional universe that they fill with multiple stories of fate, lust, and all things feminine. The stories can range from silly rated-G tales to sexually graphic XXX prose.

From TGstories.com to Literotica.com to Fictionmania.tv, the Internet is a hotbed for those who want to immerse themselves into the worlds of femme fiction. I read somewhere on Facebook that just one of these sites claimed over one million subscribers!

Some sites are dedicated to graphic novelization and the comic book format. There are amateur animations and more mainstream hentai (a subgenre of Japanese manga and animation that is characterized by overtly sexualized characters and sexually explicit images and plots). Eastern cultures celebrate transgender identities, transitioning characters, and female cartoons characters with a *little something extra* much more than Western Cultures. In America, though, all you have to do is go to Amazon.com for proof of the dozens of entries of crossdressing erotica.

For men who are struggling with their gender identities, or girlfriends or wives who are on a desperate search for enlightenment about their crossdressing partners, a quick search for the word "crossdressing" will quickly reinforce your preconceived notions that crossdressing is a fetish.

For Your Consideration ~

> *Many crossdressers enjoy the erotica that authors, graphic artists, and animators have created. It allows the crossdresser to escape to worlds where they don't have to take responsibility for who they are, where they can magically become a woman without the worry of permanence. You know, what most literature and entertainment is meant to do for the average Joe and Jane.*

> *Isn't it pornography, you ask?*

> *Some of it is, of course. Some of it is erotica. And some of it is just decent literature or filmmaking. I believe the downfall of pornography comes when the reader or watcher starts to insist that the worlds of make believe are what real life should be. It should be relegated to the realms of fantasy, not usurp reality.*

Forced Feminization ~~not Part~~

Forced feminization allows the man to be absolved from the responsibility of acknowledging their desires of crossdressing. If they are *forced* to do it, it's the dominant partner's responsibility for putting the crossdresser into that situation. The crossdresser is off the hook for being held responsible, able to maintain their masculinity with the thought that their feminization was beyond their control.

There are also many sites dedicated to forced feminization and forced femme makeovers. There exists comportment and sissy schools where dominant females make their clients become obedient maidservants for however long the client's Visa card has paid.

Drag Queens And Kings

RuPaul is the most famous face of drag queens. The show she hosts, *RuPaul's Drag Race*, is what most people with basic cable or Internet access understand drag queens to be. He has been classic in his individuality and a proponent of establishing a counter-culture all his own.

But he is just one of many drag queens who have come before him. Other notable famous drag queens – including Divine, Dame Edna Everage, and Danny La Rue – have all made successful mainstream careers as drag entertainers.

One of the popular misconceptions about drag queens is that they are all gay. While I won't postulate supposed census percentages, many take on their female personas strictly as a form of self-exploration or performance art. Some look at their feminine facades as a statement of self-expression, whether for personal or public purposes.

While RuPaul represents the perfection of *high drag*, many others use "drag" as part of their everyday life. Remember in the 80s and 90s when the emo Goth look was so prevalent? There were plenty of young men using eyeliner, mascara and lipstick as part of their look. That practice would be considered a form of drag by some standards.

And don't forget that women can also portray a masculine persona. Many female entertainers work as drag kings to emulate popular male stars like the late Elvis Presley or Michael Jackson. Others pursue careers as comedians or in performance troupes. Julie Andrews herself had a successful run on Broadway (and in the film) in the starring role in Victor/Victoria.

For Your Consideration ~

Why is it socially acceptable by both men and women that a woman emulates the masculine form, while a man doing the same for the feminine form is frowned upon? We see heterosexual women, everyday, dressed in masculine clothing, for the office or for comfort. In fact, it is much more acceptable for women to dress in male cut clothing and wear their hair in a more severe male style cut.

Katherine Hepburn is a wonderful example of the modern woman, before it was acceptable to be so. She was a fierce independent woman who shocked America with her non-conforming practice of wearing pants. Nowadays, most women wear pants, leggings, or stretch jeans and nobody pays them any mind.

Annie Lenox, the famous international singer and artist, made a habit of wearing short pixie hair and very masculine attire. She was and is considered an amazing talent and a fashion innovator, not a crossdresser.

Dress And Release

There is a cross-section (no pun intended) of men who dress for one reason, and one reason only. How shall I put this? They like to get all dolled up as a pretty princess so that they can have a happily-ever-after... dress as a sexy secretary so that they can take a final dictation for the day... put on a French Maid uniform so that they can dust off the stove pipe. If you still are confused by my analogies, let me be more straightforward. Some crossdressing men dress solely for the purpose of masturbation.

Whatever the article of clothing – whether just a pair of panties, pantyhose, or a more complete ensemble – these men love to feel and see what they are wearing. They love to imagine themselves as a woman that would wear these clothes.

Those sometimes taboo feelings and thoughts of femininity excite them and drive them to... take care of business south of the border. After the act is complete and the excitement subsides, those feelings are typically replaced with a sense of shame. The man would want to clean up, undress, and put those bad things away where they found them or keep them hidden.

For Your Consideration ~

If a boy discovers crossdressing during adolescence and puberty, it can easily become part of their self-pleasure routine. The desire to become a female with the aid of the chosen clothing, in and of itself is a sensual and forbidden experiment. Looking in the mirror and seeing that emerging female façade creates butterflies and sexual tension. If these boys had a proclivity to sexual release primarily through the act of feminine dressing, they can fall into repeated feminine dressing as an adulthood fetish. If a boy crossdresses prior to their sexual self-discovery during puberty, then it was not the only driver for their eventual sexual identity.

Crossplay / Cosplay

The term cosplay mean "costume play". It is not torrid. It is the activity or practice of dressing up as a character from a work of fiction (such as a comic book, video game, literature, or television show). The act has become more mainstream as people have embraced comics and sci-fi as part of pop culture.

Crossplay is defined as dressing in a costume as the opposite sex. In these cases, a man dresses as an established female character such as Wonder Woman and Ms. Marvel or gender-bending a traditionally male character into a female Joker or a Ms. Punisher (although these characters already exist in the DC and Marvel universe, respectively... don't get me started 'cause I could geek out all day about it!).

I have dressed as some of my favorite male and female comic superheroes. I have even coaxed my girlfriend into dressing as a heroine or villain or anti-heroine for the last few comic book conventions. Score! She looks amazing every year!

The practice started initially as people dressed as their favorite Japanese anime or manga character, and has grown faster than a speeding bullet into all segments of pop culture (Dr. Who, Star Trek, Star Wars, Marvel, DC, and more!). I have seen many girls dress up as any of a number of Doctors from the Doctor Who series. Are they considered crossdressers? No! They just love the characters so much they want to honor them.

My girlfriend told me that she felt different and empowered as the character she was dressed as. It was strange for some people to see Spider-Man's Black Cat walk down a New York City sidewalk, but my girlfriend pulled it off in grand fashion.

I also walked down the same street dressed in a black bodysuit with a lightning bolt emblazoned on my ample chest, with long blond hair, a mask, long gloves and thigh high boots with five-inch heels. At that moment, I was not Savannah but the character I had chosen to emulate. It was less about crossdressing and took on a different form of artistic expression. I was paying homage to that character and wanted to do all I could to respect her.

Interestingly, I have found myself shying away from cosplaying male characters up until recent years. I always felt more comfortable as a female character, even though it takes a lot of work to emulate the female form (with padding, breast forms, and corsetry). I actually have found that I have a skewed sense of self as a man, thinking that I am physically inadequate.

Living with Crossdressing: Defining a New Normal

For Your Consideration ~

> *People come in all shapes and sizes – tall, thin, short, and stocky – and many want to dress up as their favorite character. Regardless of a specific body shape, remember that comic books have exaggerated the human form for years and most proportions are unattainable. If people want to pay homage to their favorite character in their own artistic way, please remember that it takes confidence and courage to dress up, and to own their portrayal with their heads held high.*

Escape Artists

[handwritten note: maby? I need to explore/think about this aspect a little more]

Life is stressful. It's a rat race. The corporate world is dog-eat-dog. Like Rick Springfield sang, *I'm working hard, I don't know why, I'm like a working class dog, and I just get by*. The only two things guaranteed in life are death and taxes.

Many of us come home from a hard day of work. I know this is not a purely masculine concept, especially in the new millennium. I have seen strong women, one in particular who works a full career while raising three children, endure as much, if not more, stress than many men. But I must speak of the men for this type of crossdresser.

Some men have a need to come home after an especially stressful 12- to 14-hour workday and dress in something pretty. There is not necessarily a sexual component as described in the Dress and Release section above. What occurs is a subtle shift in cognitive reality. While embodying the same body, the act of dressing as a woman allows the man to be like Alice in

Wonderland. He can escape down the rabbit hole into a land of make believe.

Comforted by the tight confining pantyhose and soft cashmere sweater – maybe with full makeup and wig, maybe not – the man becomes a woman who does not share the same problems as her male counterpart. Johnny Depp, in Tim Burton's semi-biographical film *Ed Wood*, illustrated this concept better than I can explain it. For an hour or an evening, the female persona can stride around to wash dishes, watch television, or go for a walk or drive without ever considering or worrying about the outstanding dilemmas of *his* day-to-day life.

Why can't these people just relieve stress the old-fashioned way? You know, going for a jog or working out?

For Your Consideration ~

You may believe it unlikely that an article of clothing can change how you think. According to some studies, clothing can affect how you feel about yourself, in general.

Most crossdressers may not even know why the act of crossdressing makes them calmer and more at ease. But since they have a desire to dress in the first place, the stress of not dressing may cause more tension. Putting on a blouse and skirt allows them to feel complete, letting them approach something close to normalcy, as far as they understand it. Crossdressers who deny their needs will tend to feel off when forced to curb their behavior to the conformities of what is considered acceptable.

For both men and women, ask yourself... when you change into baggy tops, jeans or an oversized sweatshirt at the end of the day, aren't you comforted by them? Weren't you desperate to slip into those clothes that represented relaxation? The world hasn't changed. The situations and stresses of the days haven't gone away. But, wearing the comfy clothes somehow changed your perception of the events.

Experimenters

There will always be men who just want to engage in the act of dressing in women's lingerie or panties as an exhilarating experiment in the bedroom with their partners. This is not something that will necessarily become a fetish or a gateway moment leading to full-blown crossdressing (or worse, in the female partner's fearful eyes, transitioning to womanhood). Of course, only a man who is comfortable with this type of exploration of the feminine will be likely to participate.

Be advised that men are not always the ones to bring up this idea for bedroom play. Female partners have been known to bring it up to their men, whether as a scenario to humiliate, dominate or feminize their spouse/partner. Also know, ladies, that most men want to please their women (and happen to enjoy sex, too!) and would be agreeable to most bedroom play if approached in the right way.

For Your Consideration ~

Remember that communication with your partner is the most important tool in your relationship toolbox. We are all filled

Living with Crossdressing: Defining a New Normal

> with some degree of fear and expectations as it comes to our needs and desires. We assume our partners will react a certain way to us based on our own expectations and experience.
>
> Communication is a skill to be developed. To whatever degree you can master this verbal art form, it will allow you to clothe yourself in honesty about what you consider important to your own growth and well-being.

Bedroom play is not the only place that men may want to explore their femininity without a deeper motivation in place. It is said that Halloween is the crossdressers' Christmas, the one night of the year that a man can explore his feminine side under public scrutiny and be able to explain it away as parody or art. Yes, it is true that crossdressers have used Halloween to introduce their feminine sides to the world. Most men, however, simply dress up as a female character for fun or as part of a gender-bending couple's costume concept.

For More of Your Consideration ~

> Why do some girls and women dress up as slutty nurses, sexy witches, and more? Is it because that is what the costume manufacturers and society have dictated for us? Halloween is a holiday to abandon that who you are in favor of a persona more exaggerated or opposite than what we consider normal.
>
> I do not recall there being a problem or stray thought the next day when a female office mate decided to dress up as Charlie Chaplin. But if a man dressed as Marilyn Monroe at the same

office party, there could be some whispering about his motivations. Stigma exists that the man must be gay or a crossdresser (and they just don't know it yet!) if they present themselves successfully as the "weaker" sex.

Princesses, Brides, Fairies And More

Princesses, brides, secretaries, maids, and fairies show up on the same list. What do they represent and have in common? What was the list originally asking for? Will Alex Trebek famously ask you to put your answer in the form of a question? Give up?

I will not keep you in suspense any longer, dear reader. For the crossdresser, the above list represents the same thing it does for most young girls, power or ultimate femininity.

But wait, Savannah, being a secretary or a maid was never on my little girl list of what I wanted to be when I grew up. I wanted to be the first female president!

Yes. You are right, of course. The list is an exaggeration of femininity based on what we have come to accept as the social norm for women. As far as we have come in equality between the sexes, there is still a divide that traditionally separates men and women. Expectations still rule most thinking.

Women still are expected to wear an expensive white flowing dress on their wedding day. My girlfriend, however, is through with the whole concept. Once is enough! Some little girls still want Disney Princess dresses to wear around the house (and sometimes to the grocery store with mom). Accessorizing with sparkled wings and a wand lets the little girl soar as high as her imagination allows.

But you haven't properly answered my question, Savannah!

Living with Crossdressing: Defining a New Normal

I know.

Yes, I presented secretaries and maids as part of my list. And I will answer the question with a question. Why do most little girls gravitate toward Fisher Price kitchen sets, Barbie Dream Houses, and Disney Princesses? Sure, you could say that it's about the massive push for advertising, but the marketing is geared that way because it works! Focus groups and marketing research has proven that little girls want what they want just like little boys want what they want. Girls want dolls and boys want Legos (I love, love, love my Legos!) So what does that all mean?

All it means to a crossdresser is that there are typically female dominated roles that, as a man, we cannot fulfill. *Leave it to Beaver*'s June Cleaver cleaned the house and prepared family dinners in her dress and pearls. Women have the honor of walking down the aisle in a white satin and lace wedding gown.

Some crossdressers want to emulate these female roles. Stepping into these stereotypes give them that feeling of femininity, triggering synopses in their brain through tactile memory and wish fulfillment to believe themselves to be a woman. Men could never be brides. But as their feminine self, they can become one through the simple act of donning the attire.

For Your Consideration ~

> *There is a fine line between being engulfed in the experience of the bride, the maid, the housewife or the secretary, and being drawn to, for example, the PVC or rubber-clad French maid as a fetish. Ladies, if your partner is engaged almost exclusively in one of these femme personas, please start the dialogue to discuss his motivations. While crossdressers and*

fetishists share some similar feminine fantasies and wish fulfillments, the non-fetish crossdresser typically gravitates toward more appropriate clothing for private and public use while the fetishist will be found in their attire of choice regardless of the event or situation.

Sybil Dressers

Remember that television movie, *Sybil*? Sally Fields portrayed a woman with multiple personalities; each not aware of the others packed into her mindscape. Each existed as a fracture of Sybil's psyche, there to protect her main identity. *Some of it seems like medical hokum*, you might say. I am not here to speculate the validity of medical science or documented cases.

I am here to tell you that, like in the Escape Artists section, there is a distinct shift in thinking for some crossdressers when dressed. For myself, I have more confidence to dance! Yes, as silly as it may sound, I am very self-conscious about my dancing abilities as a man (I know, hard to believe!). But let me get on my LBD and knee length boots – and put on that song that makes me squeal, "That's my jam!" – and I'm racing to the dance floor to shake my *groove thang*. And, yes, dear reader, I can move pretty well in my favorite 4-inch heels.

But enough about me.

There are some men who dress to de-stress, letting the cares of the workday and the rat race slip away as they slide on their favorite pair of pantyhose. They go about their business, whatever that may be when they dress, enjoying the escape, comfort, and distance that their dressing persona provides. But there are others who have a female identity, in part, out of necessity to protect themselves from the rigors, turmoil, and torment that they have suffered in their male lives. Whether it is from mental or physical abuse as a youth or from a lifetime of denial or depression, the female persona can serve as a dissociative identity for the man. The man can be gruff and unhappy, while the female side is more reserved and content. Where the male side is quick to anger, the female persona is patient and cool.

It does seem strange that the clothes would make the difference, but the feminine things for these crossdressing men are the catalysts to invoke the comforting half... the desired half... the better half. Like Billy Batson speaking the word *Shazam!* to become the super-powered Captain Marvel, these men *become* the women, in mind and spirit, to combat and quell the voices and instincts they grew up with.

For Your Consideration ~

> *Just because the crossdressing male uses his female persona to become a softer, well-adjusted and balanced individual (both physically and mentally) it doesn't mean that he wants to transition to the opposite sex. Femininity can be an escape and a method of presentation of an elusive intangible quality that only Gaia (Mother Earth) would understand.*

The Tactile-tician [handwritten: I think this is a large part of it 4 me, but ~~tactile~~ touch + sight]

What does this somewhat made up term mean to me? Yeah, I made it up. I couldn't find it in the urban dictionary anywhere. Based on the Latin word *tactilis*, to be tactile is to be connected to the sense of touch.

Living with Crossdressing: Defining a New Normal

So what?

Well, women have it so much better than men in the general clothing department. They have so much more variety in the workplace, while their male counterparts get to wear a suit... or, maybe, a suit. What a choice! If it is a business casual environment, men get to wear dress pants and a dress shirt... maybe even [gasp] a Polo shirt. Wow! Of course, if I had all sorts of money and better fashion sense, I would have access to finer materials.

The crossdresser craves soft things, shiny and smooth things, the feel of a soft material that slides across the skin, clings in the right places, caresses and compresses like a tight cocoon. Women who wear pantyhose for work can't wait to strip them off when they get home. The crossdressing man longs to keep these items on, to feel them on his body. Some of it may be due to the infrequency of their ability to dress, but the feeling of shaving our legs, drying off and slipping on a pair of pantyhose or stockings is an utterly exhilarating exercise. The way the air flows across the fabric and skin as we walk, the way the fabric encases our limbs, the way the nylon feels when we stroke (get your mind out of the gutter, ladies and gentlemen!) our hands along our thighs and calves.

Because there is an expectation of women to wear certain articles, I personally believe that some have lost that loving feeling about wearing those clothes. For most ladies, clothing has become a utilitarian process of adornment and disrobing. Somewhat lost is the art of *becoming*. Yes, I believe that with time some have forgotten about the sensations of the fabrics worn. My girlfriend picks out blouses and tops because she loves the way they feel through her fingers. But once purchased and worn a few times, does she consciously continue to take a moment to appreciate what she is wearing? Jen says, "yes." Does she stop to look in the mirror to realize the power of her clothing? Jen says, "Realize the power of what I am wearing? Nope!"

Crossdressing men continue to appreciate the clothes they select and wear. For the crossdressing male, clothing has power. A pair of pantyhose encases the legs, making them feel more feminine and shimmery. A satin top is soft and slick, evoking a sensual wrap of protection. A skirt or a dress, unique to women in modern society (except those Scotsmen's kilts), screams out its womanly roots!

For Your Consideration ~

If you're a partner of a crossdressing man, do yourself (and your partner) a favor and be a part of their ritualistic process of becoming their female personas. I understand that it may be difficult to see your partner in the various levels of completion. I understand to see him without makeup or hair while he already has a blouse and skirt on may be disconcerting and somewhat off-putting. It can be visually strange and foreign.

Try to keep a level of objectivity and watch his process of becoming. Of course, crossdressing males will have various degrees of practice and knowledge as it comes to make-up application and selection. So, the process may take a while. But watch how he treats his body and the care and effort he puts into the process. Pantyhose, hip and butt padding, corsetry and body briefers, tucking of the nether region, breast forms of some sort, the outer clothing, the make-up application, the wig (if needed), and the shoes.

I heard from one woman that she "was resentful" that her husband took "over an hour to get ready", while she "was ready in 15 minutes". What she realized is that she had lost the appreciation for the clothing she wore and for the process of becoming. Her husband's dressing had "shamed her" into paying more attention to her own femininity.

We crossdressing males can be fixated on the perfection of female identities and our presentation. We forget that women, having had to live a certain way their entire life, may take their own femininity for granted. Just like we take our manhood for granted.

These are strange days, indeed.

The Girls Next Door

If I had to put a label on myself – and I must state that I truly hate labels, both as it applies to our identities and how other people feel they need to bucket us – I would see myself in this category. Even though I have found myself in different categories over the years as I have traveled my road of self-discovery and balance (more on that later on in My Story), I see myself as just a man trying to have a normal life while becoming Savannah from time to time.

I call this group the Girls Next Door because of what the name implies. The Girl Next Door is perceived as approachable, dependable, and trustworthy. They are an archetype of a kind and unassuming woman that you are drawn to. That is all I want.

What do you want?

I want to become Savannah and be able to walk out the front door without worry of judgment or scorn from others. I tend to want to go to mainstream establishments (Starbucks, Outback Steakhouse, etc.). I try to blend in as a passable woman, not because I worry that I will be found out but because I want to enjoy life just like any other person. I try to carry myself with confidence, radiating a smile and positivity to disarm anyone that may give me stares of novelty or disdain.

The Girls Next Door strive to be stylish without being garish (unless the event calls for it… we are always up for a challenge!). If you saw them in a restaurant or on the street, you would probably have to take a second look to decide whether they were men or women. They take utmost care with their presentation and are comfortable in their skin as a woman without being completely overt with their sexuality. Trust me, we want to be as sexy as we can, but we have advanced to a more mature (not matronly – never that!) style that is alluring, practical, and appropriate for the occasion.

What could be more enjoyable than a nice evening out with friends and my girlfriend? Whether at a bar or in a club setting, a coffee shop, lounge or restaurant, I am happiest when I am validated as a true individual. I am not validated as a woman because people openly accept and embrace who I am (that I reserve for my girlfriend); I am validated when I am out and no one seems to care or shoot a second look my way. Acceptance in society for me, in particular, is when they treat me like everyone else. In NYC, that acceptance comes in the form of indifference – haha!

Living with Crossdressing: Defining a New Normal

For Your Consideration ~

Ladies, imagine a life where walking out from under the shadows of the front porch portico or from behind a rising garage door always has the opportunity to be met with scorn and hatred from the general populace because of how we are classified. We are a different lot from many in the LGBTQ community because we are more fluid in our gender. Where most on the community party list are striving for acceptance as a single gender identity, the non-transitioning crossdresser continually slides between their male and female personas.

Do you want to stay a man or become a woman?
If you only dress as a woman on occasion, you must not be very serious about it.

Crossdressers are still misunderstood as a gender group by the masses and by other transgender and transsexual groups. Most crossdressers are not looking to change their biology. They are not masquerading as woman to bait men into a torrid relationship. Because crossdressers do not follow defined rules set for other transgender or transsexual groups, they are considered an anomaly.

The problem comes in the secrecy that still surrounds our kind. While many gays, lesbians and transitioning men and women are emerging and being accepted, crossdressers are a mostly hidden faction still considered to be fetishists and part timers.

Tranvestic Fetishism

The people diagnosed – also a pet peeve of mine as science and the medical field continuously consider many of us crossdressers as suffering from one of many disorders – with Tranvestic Fetishism must include two key criteria. The first is that the individual (man or woman) must be sexually aroused by the act of crossdressing. The second is that the individual must experience significant distress or impairment (at work, socially, privately, in their relationships, etc.) as a result of their behavior.

Types of fetishism include, but are not limited to, persons that collect specific types of lingerie, stockings or pantyhose, bridal gowns, sissy dresses, and the like in order to achieve sexual climax and satisfaction. They have more of an obsessive-compulsive need to dress in a very specific way to gain a very specific result.

Please be aware that Transvestic Fetishism is different from the pre-adolescent crossdressing boy who is discovering *her* as hormones rage during his sexual awakening, or the adult male who suddenly finds himself attracted to women's clothing for the first time. These examples of *new girls* are trying to understand their identity and will most likely be initially sexually aroused by the experience. Only those who dress strictly for the desire of arousal would be designated into the category of Transvestic Fetishism.

Infants, Baby Girls, and Sissies

There are some men who like to regress to a child-like state of innocence. Some like to wear diapers under their male clothing. I have seen men who seem to enjoy the risk of being discovered in

Living with Crossdressing: Defining a New Normal

public by having the diaper's edges on display. Maybe they enjoy how the diapers feel. Maybe they are looking for that vague primal tactile sensation from their infancy.

Some like to dress in frilly panties and petticoats with bows in their hair, acting like little pre-adolescent girls or their approximation of what they think little girls should act like. There is sometimes a regression to a simpler era when dresses and proper childish comportment was expected.

Bearded Ladies

Like the infants and sissies in the previous section, this group's motivation is also foreign to me. Men who dress as women but do not try to hide their facial hair are sometimes labeled as genderqueer. They don't conform to conventional gender distinctions, but identify with neither or a combination of male and female genders. They take on the attributes of both sexes in an amalgam for their presentation. I guess the Bearded Lady at the early- and mid-20th century sideshows could have been considered genderqueer, as well.

I can only share a single personal experience. During a private transgender event, I noticed a bearded man in a satin evening gown. In a sad irony, I found that his persona put me off because he *offended* my sensibilities as to what a transgender male should be. Maybe the beard was not part of what he wanted as his feminine personae? Maybe, in his home life, the shaving of the beard would have been too shocking and raise too many eyebrows?

There could be one of a dozen reasons why this individual chose to wear both a dress and facial hair. I will never know his true intent. I felt bad that I rushed to judgment about him without knowing more about him. As he moves forward on his own journey, I can only hope to wish him well.

For Your Consideration ~

Crossdressing men may keep from taking their female presentation to the fullest degree because they're concerned about what others may think or say about them as men. For example, some crossdressers detest the hair on their body because it keeps them from being able to wear more revealing clothing, but keep from manscaping because friends or co-workers may ask why they do so.

Some partners see the deconstruction of what they consider male as a warning sign of the ghosts of transitioning future. Shaving one's body could be considered a gateway to other, more permanent, body changes. Partners may worry that they will be forced to defend against questions about our appearance and behavior by friends and family.

And don't forget, crossdressers, most partners don't really want to run up against your prickly body three days after you have shaved or see their man with less hair than them. Many women find it hard to see a smooth shaved man because they equate masculinity with body hair. Body hair + Man = Normal

Be mindful of both perspectives!

Land Of Confusion

Now I am more confused than I was at the beginning of reading this chapter, you groan. *Thanks for nothing, Ms. Hauk!*
I know. I know.

The reality of the situation you find yourself in, as a crossdresser or a partner of a crossdresser, is that there is a vast gender identity spectrum out there that has been generalized and boiled down to the simple label of crossdressing or the more clinical medical description transvestism.

If you imagine the Empire State Building in the heart of Manhattan, each floor could be seen as a type of crossdressing or transgender expression. The subways and garages are on the lowest levels, maybe to represent the closeted and private fetishists since they are very much still considered the community underground. Then you hop on the escalator to the main concourses where the glitzy shops serve as an analogy for the flamboyant and over-the-top drag queens and high art performers. Now that you are done shopping, you figure you better get to work on the 18th floor. Most people have little idea what corporations and companies operate in the leased office spaces throughout the building. They operate fairly autonomously and under the radar because it's just business as usual for the typical non-fetish, non-transitioning crossdressing male.

But what about the observation deck, Savannah. Isn't that where every crossdresser wants to go?

That is a great question... and fear.

The average crossdresser aims to perfect their craft of feminine illusion. We do the best we can with the makeup skills we learn, the corsets and padding we can buy, and the fashions we can acquire. Sure, we dream a fantasy where, for a moment, we imagine stepping out onto the observation deck as a fully realized and accepted woman, but I'm not willing to pay those prices to ride the elevator up to the top floor every day. Heck no! I enjoy my duality of being able to operate in life as a man (for most of the time) and as a woman (when the feeling strikes).

I like my parts just the way they are, thank you very much!

So, if you like your parts that God gave you at birth, why do you feel the need to crossdress as a woman in the first place?

Let's try to figure that out together, my dear reader.

Why We Do It

> *For the past 33 years, I have looked in the mirror every morning and asked myself: 'If today were the last day of my life, would I want to do what I am about to do today?' And whenever the answer has been 'No' for too many days in a row, I know I need to change something.*
>
> ~ Steve Jobs

Introduction

Why do we do it?

It's an age-old question that most crossdressers started asking when they first realized that they were not like everyone else. But what *is* it to be like everyone else?

People who crossdress cover all nationalities, ethnicities, religions, economic classes, and has been reported (not sure how) to affect one out of every ten men. They can be the pizza delivery guy, your mail courier, your doctor, judges, senators... your partner.

I can describe the need to crossdress by comparing it to a crying baby and their security blanket. Yes, dear readers, we crossdressers are just a bunch of babies! Wink! Seriously, though, think about a toddler who is dropped into a new location. They are out of place and scared. They start fidgeting and crying, unable to process the feelings of disconnect, fear and stress. But if you give them their favorite blanky (that's a blanket for all the singles out there), they calm down and are comforted by its familiar texture, smell, and softness. You will find the child with its arms wrapped around that blanket with nary a care in the world.

The urge to crossdress is something altogether different but yet the same as the example of the security blanket. Whatever the root reasons is to why we have the urge to dress, the result is that we are comforted by the feelings we get when we do so. It is transformative to our state of mind. I won't say that the act of dressing changes the chemicals in our brain, but I will say that it does shift our perceptions in some measure.

When I grew up, it was very evident in our household that it was frowned upon for a boy to want to play with his sister's Barbie dolls. But it was certainly okay to play with the 12" (again, keep your minds out of the gutter, please) Adventure Team Commander GI Joe action figure. If we started calling Dream House Barbie an action figure, would it be okay for boys to play with them?

Boys play with trucks, jeeps and toy guns; girls play with dolls, wear princess dresses, and cook in their Easy Bake ovens. Sure, we are hard-wired to want certain things. I know of a four-year-old girl who begged her parents for a plastic stacked washer and dryer set for Christmas. The parents were puzzled but bought the item as one of their daughter's gifts from Santa. Was that request based on the fact that the little girl wanted to emulate what she saw her mother do? If a little boy were to make that same request, would it have been granted?

In today's child rearing, what is considered traditional and gender-specific social norms? I understand that the modern parent is more educated and aware of gender identification and preference, even as it affects children as young as three or four-years-old. But in my era (I'm a Gen X-er, I will leave it at that) there was no World Wide Web to educate our parents about a young boy who has an attraction to wearing his sister's clothes. Anything we did find out about crossdressing was considered forbidden underground erotica, fetish, and taboo.

How could we consider ourselves normal in the face of what information or support was available? Wait... I think I may have walked off on a tangent. Let's get to back to the question of why do we do it.

Let's try this again.

The asking of the question at all is to assume that the question needs to be answered. Is it the crossdresser's job to explain to you why he is the way he is, especially when he most likely will not fully understand the reasons why himself? Will any answer satisfy the question of the root cause?

Is an answer required because the crossdresser is not considered normal and, because of that, his condition needs to have an explanation in order for those around him to be able to cast a defense around it? Are crossdressers not normal? I didn't realize that. I always felt normal, but thank you for letting me know.

So there is a cure for me, then?

If we look back into the history of fashion we can see that our Founding Fathers all wore dapper clothing, knee socks and white powdered wigs. Royalty, throughout the ages, is depicted in drawings and paintings as being draped in satins, silks and other fineries, powdered faces and wigs that could be considered close to the modern interpretation of what male cross-dressing is. And if I ran into William Wallace and his Celtic broadsword from *Braveheart*, I don't think I would point out the absurdity of his kilt.

They can take our kilts, but they can't take our manhood!

I'm paraphrasing, of course.

Living with Crossdressing: Defining a New Normal

For me, it goes back to the idea that the clothing makes the man or woman. Who decides what is socially acceptable... that men only wear suits and women only wear dresses? I see plenty of women wearing jeans and pants at work and at home. I guess they are all crossdressing females. I didn't realize I was in such good company!

I am being sarcastic, of course, but I do feel there is a severe double standard when it comes to the acceptability of clothing. I mean, there are entire lines of clothing made for women geared toward the idea of *borrowing the boyfriend's shirt* or boy short underwear. Even the limited fashion men do have has been commandeered by woman's fashion! Other than the Speed-o swim trucks, I can't think of any current fashion that slants a feminine style to male clothing other than more fashionable colors and some fabrics.

But, Savannah! We're not talking about speedos and kilts! We're talking about our husbands and boyfriends wearing our bras and panties and using our makeup to look like a woman!

Thank you, dear reader, for bringing me back to the topic at hand. Based on the types of crossdressers discussed earlier (and I know I only scratched the surface of the entire crossdressing spectrum), there are a few reasons that men have a desire to dress as the fairer sex. One, they find that dressing as a woman provides an escape from their version of reality. Two, some are trying to fulfill a part of their psyche with the physical expression of femininity. Lastly, some use the sexuality of dressing as a means to fulfill a fantasy and experience a sexual high. There are many more reasons, to be sure. All I can hope is to bring illumination to the *whys* of the non-transitioning non-fetish crossdresser. There is obviously an urge to dress that needs to be addressed.

It is a highly sensual experience, if not a completely sexual one. The act of focusing on the clothes and how they feel on the body, the way the makeup changes our male appearance, the act of *becoming* is highly sensual. It is a sensory experience that takes in all of the senses over the entire body, not just the erogenous zone between our legs.

Crossdressing boys may have gravitated to their mother's or sister's bureaus or dressers. The fabrics and the articles themselves fascinated them. They wondered what it would feel like to put on a pair of underwear, a slip or pair of dress heels. It didn't matter that the clothing or shoes were too big. It only mattered how the clothing felt through their fingers, how the clothing felt on them, and how wearing the clothing made them feel. There could be physical excitement before and during the experience. There may have been regret or shame afterward, either because of being in a place that is considered off-limits or the taboo of the act.

As an adult, introduction to the world of crossdressing can come in many forms. An urge component is involved. Sometimes a crossdressing male is introduced to the life by coaxing or accident. Sometimes (like what you hear when watching episodes of *Criminal Minds*) there is a stressor event. And sometimes a man just stops denying those urges that had been suppressed from a lifetime of shame and mainstream non-acceptance.

I have a close crossdressing friend, Victoria, that may never have realized her true nature if it hadn't been for a former cis-girlfriend asking her to try on a pair of panties as something to spice up their love life. Since the act of crossdressing was supportive inside the relationship, it became normal for them. They eventually broke up, unfortunately, but those acts inside the relationship prompted Victoria to better understand his new urges.

Living with Crossdressing: Defining a New Normal

That first pair of panties led to a second (and more), providing the first steps upon a path of self-discovery.

He now lives with a foot (or heel) in both worlds. He is comfortable with having both a male and female identity. He lives and works as his male self, and gets dressed up as Victoria when he has extra time to go to the mall, into the city, or just to lounge around the house.

And do you know what makes him sad? The simple fact that there is still a huge divide in America where it seems almost impossible to believe that he could find and have a relationship with a cisgender woman who would accept and support who he is as both a man and a woman.

He did use social media to make a subtle proclamation of who *she* is. He put it out there for the digital world to see. The people who actually read Facebook posts instead of just looking at the pictures have been accepting of *her*.

So what have we learned?

Are we enlightened about why men like to dress as women?

According to varying reports (and, of course, I am scratching my wigged head in wonder as to how the forthcoming statistic was captured in census format), there could be up to 150 million transgender persons in the world. Of course, that statistic puts all trans-related persons in the same bucket. And since crossdressers are probably the most secretive (alright… I'll say it… the most 'in the closet'), I find it unlikely that a true cross-section could have been allotted; that the reported numbers are lower than the true count.

At the end of the day, the reasons for *why* we crossdress may never be satisfactory to our friends, our family, our partners or even us. It's like if we finally found out how the dead returned to life in George Romero's classic film, *The Night of the Living Dead*. If we knew for sure it was a result of the space satellite named Wormwood, would we be satisfied with the root cause? How many of you were up in arms with how *Lost* ended?

The point is that understanding the *whys* is, many times, not helpful to our partners. The explanation would be heard, but may not truly understood. Can anyone who is not gay understand the psychology of why a man is attracted to a man or a woman to a woman? Can a *normie* or civilian understand the alcoholic mind? I can walk a mile in my partner's heels, but she will still roll her eyes wondering why I want to keep them on all night while she would have taken them off in the first half-hour of the wedding reception.

Each crossdressing man's motivations are as individualized as grains of sand on a beach. Unless there is a battery of therapy in which we truly open ourselves up for inspection, many of us will never know the reasons why we have a need to dress. And because every crossdresser's journey is different – each a result from a mix of psychology, experience, genetics, environment and other drivers – there is no pat answer. Not in this book or any book.

In Closing

All I can ask of you, dear loving and supportive partner is to listen to your man's story and ask questions in an honest and open way (trying to keep judgment and fear from the questions you ask and the answers you hear). I understand this discovery and the learning process can be of the utmost difficulty. The situation is just as difficult for the crossdresser. There is a human need to anticipate possible future threats. We know the dynamics of the relationship has changed. How you think about our gender will never be the same.

The bell has been rung. And can't be unrung.

You are filled with fear. So are we. That is truly something that both the crossdresser and their partner share.

We fear your rejection. We fear that you will cast us out for the human beings you have discovered we are, reinforcing the belief that we are freaks of nature – something to be feared and treated with disgust. Something abnormal, something debased, something filled with perversion.

You are afraid that we encompass all those things I just mentioned. You fear that if we have lied about this part of our life, what else have we kept from you? You fear that this discovery is a gateway moment that will lead to us wanting to become a woman full-time or to become attracted to men. The world you have built and have grown accustomed to is on the verge of collapse.

But is it? Is your world about to implode? Is that the truth? Yes, something of a serious nature has fundamentally changed between the two of you. There is no mistake about that. I am not absurd enough to try to dissuade you of that fact. But this discovery does not have to be a death sentence.

It will take work. It will take humility and understanding. It will take a concerted effort from your crossdresser to not be defensive or feel a sense of entitlement. Remember, crossdresser, that your partner is a brand new visitor to a world in which you have lived all your life (or a significant part of it).

Be open. Be honest. Be supportive and understanding. Clean away the thorns and underbrush from the past and start rebuilding that solid foundation between the two of you. Crossdressers, you have to be as understanding and supportive of your spouse as you hope her to be of you.

Partners, start asking questions of your crossdressing man.

What questions? I'm in such shock right now that I can't think of anything to ask beyond, 'Are you gay?'.

Ok. So I will get you started with a slow-pitch softball lob easy question... ahem... Hun, how long have you being dressing this way?

Lifers And Late Bloomers

> *I have to remind myself that some birds aren't meant to be caged. Their feathers are just too bright. And when they fly away, the part of you that knows it was a sin to lock them up does rejoice. But still, the place you live in is that much more grey.*
> ~ Ellis "Red" Redding from *The Shawshank Redemption*

Realizations

Some crossdressing men, like me, have been dressing since we were very young, realizing we were different as early as five- or six-years-old. That is not to say that we stopped identifying as a boy in favor of wanting to be a girl. We just started to feel an attraction to the clothing of the opposite sex, even before there was an understanding of a possible sexual component.

On the other end of the spectrum is the group of men who realized their crossdressing tendencies only in adulthood. For these men, their discovery of wanting to dress in feminine attire usually surfaces well into their twenties. If this is not the case, there is usually a stressor or some act that introduces crossdressing to them.

The Lifers

The man who I am designating the Lifer found the allure of feminine clothing at an early pre-adolescent age. Whether from an inkling of self-discovery (sneaking into mom's room to see what treasures awaited in her dresser drawer) or stemming from an experience brought on by a friend or family member (sisters thought it would be hilarious to dress their little brother in their old dresses), these boys discovered that wearing feminine clothing was interesting and enjoyable. They found comfort in the clothing. It just *felt* right.

I'm sure they were getting off on the experience!

That comment is an adult concept. Even in this modern digital era, where we are bombarded with information and stimuli, a child wouldn't typically think about gender identities in the way an adult does. An example to illustrate this is when a little boy tries on mom's dress heels because his big sister is parading around in another pair. Other than environmental exposures (family life, television, etc.), children don't think about their gender in the same terms as adults. Many times, parents project their own life experiences, fears and stigmas onto their children's behavior. A boy doesn't *know* that he is not supposed to wobble around in mom's shoes. The innocence and wonder children enjoy – and that adults envy – should allow for the discovery of one's self. An individual will gravitate to their true nature, if given enough latitude and underlying support.

But I don't want my child to be a crossdresser.

Please remember that all little boys who dress up in girl clothes or shoes at playtime do not all have a want to crossdress. As a parent, though, would you force your child to write right-handed if

Living with Crossdressing: Defining a New Normal

you found them trying to scrawl their names in block letters with a crayon with their left? Social acceptability and standards are inflicted on us at an early age, even if we try to embrace that which makes us different.

As crossdressing boys, we have an inherent understanding that we need to keep our adventures to ourselves. The need for secrecy stems from the fact that we have been told that we shouldn't be rifling through other family members' dresser drawers – that mommy and daddy's room is off-limits. If our sister decided to dress us up in their Disney Princess dresses as part of our playtime together and everyone thinks its cute, we may be more open to sharing with others inside the family unit. But if we are shamed or made fun of while participating with our siblings, we quickly realize we need to veil our enthusiasm and to find the act as inappropriate and unacceptable.

Hence the roots of the stigma take hold. As crossdressing children, we become adept at keeping this component of our lives separate from others. We steal moments when we find ourselves alone, frantically dressing in mom's dressy heels (that she never wears anymore), her girdles and slips, or in our big sister's leotards, swimsuits or other desirables.

As we grow into adolescence and puberty, the sexual component arrives. Our hormones rage and we start to understand the physical differences between boys and girls. Our erupting attraction for girls compounds our *need* to dress and to become that desirable feminine self. There are reports and studies that state that adolescent crossdressing self-promotes its need on the individual.

How so?

As a teenager, while those aforementioned boy hormones are taking over all of his critical thinking, the act of crossdressing will typically lead to self-exploration, the rise of excitement in the private areas, and to the eventual act of masturbation. The release after masturbation is the reward for the risk taken. The act makes you feel good. It releases Dopamine in the brain that alters your mood to a better state. All seems to be right with the world! So why would you not want to do it again?

And again.

And again.

Now we come to the fork in the road. The lifetime crossdresser survived his childhood and escalated his crossdressing as a teenager. Whether dressing in solitude or with others (could be with other crossdressers or with a girlfriend), the crossdressing male finds himself in a brand new place.

I'm an adult! I have freedom! I can do what I want!

Maybe societal pressures shape the crossdresser enough to put away those frivolous and fancy thoughts in favor of a more traditional male role. Maybe crossdressing was truly just a phase of childish experimentation, or maybe those feminine feelings come back to lead to further development. If the crossdressing male decides to continue in his exploration, his may struggle with his gender identity and now, possibly, sexual identity.

Who am I?

Am I a man?

Or am I woman trapped in a man's body?

Gender dysphoria (or gender identity disorder) is a very real struggle. Men and women facing this battle feel strongly that they are not the gender of their biology. They can experience anxiety, stress, and depression. There is confusion between the ties of their gender identity to their sexual orientation.

If you want to dress as a woman you must be attracted to men, right?

Who said that was the case? One of the biggest misconceptions for the non-fetish, non-transitioning crossdressers to dispel to their partners or family is that because they like to take on a female persona they must take on all the traits of the feminine, including the switch in their attraction to the *opposite* sex (from female to male). There is a definite and defined distinction between gender identity and sexual orientation. The two are mutually exclusive. The logic in your head would state, "IF women are attracted to men AND men like to dress as women THEREFORE men who like to dress as women must like men".

Try to keep those two concepts separate. Sure, some crossdressing men will pursue answers for both their gender identity and sexual orientation. And maybe they will realize that they are actually women trapped in a man's body. And maybe they will become transitioned women who prefer men, other women, or continue to be sexually fluid. The same could be said for the non-transitioning crossdressing man. They could be completely content with periodic feminine dressing but struggle with whether they are attracted to men, women or both.

I am so confused!

It is confusing. Adding to the mix is the fact that there is now a new term out there. Gender nonconforming (GNC) is a broader, more encompassing phrase that includes people with gender dysphoria. The term also describes individuals who are neither *only* male nor female. Think about that. A man or woman could have traits that are both masculine and feminine. So, remember that little girl you played with when you were just one of the kids in the neighborhood trying to get all the playtime in before the street lights came on? Remember that she loved to get as muddy as you and could climb trees way better than you? I think the label attached to her was that she was a tomboy. In practical terms, she would be considered gender nonconforming. Little girl tomboys are totally accepted in society. Feminine, prissy boys are not.

Is your child gender dysphoric?

- He consistently says that he is really a girl even though he is genetically a boy (or visa-versa).
- Strongly prefers friends of the opposite sex.
- Rejects the clothes, toys, and play of his assigned gender.
- Refuses to urinate in the way of his assigned gender.
- Says he wants to get rid of his genitals.
- Believes he will grow up into the opposite gender.
- Has extreme distress about his body changes during puberty.

I will come back to what happens to the lifetime crossdresser as an adult after this brief intermission from our sponsors about adult-onset crossdressing.

Late Bloomers

You would think that a man would always have known that he wanted to dress as a woman.

How could those feelings have been suppressed or denied for an entire young life? Now, at age forty-two, my husband discovers that he likes femme clothes and makeup? WTF?

Men discovering their crossdressing urges as adults may have had those same feelings as children, but chose to ignore them. It may have been the result of a male dominated household was the reason for the suppression. Maybe there wasn't a feminine presence in the house to allow for borrowing clothes for experimentation. Perhaps there was little exposure to the crossdressing culture, even if the only example was Dustin Hoffman in *Tootsie*. It's possible that they weren't aware anything was missing at all until an experience opened their eyes to the possibilities.

There are many triggers that could lead to your man deciding that wearing your bras and panties while you are at the grocery store is the right thing to do. I cannot promise that a seemingly innocent gender-bending Halloween couples costume concept will not evolve into something more frequent. But I know that a single instance of crossdressing may lead to nothing more than that one adventure, either.

If your partner discovers that crossdressing should be part of the understanding of who he is, it doesn't mean that he is, or always was, secretly homosexual. It doesn't mean this discovery will lead to plans of transitioning to womanhood or the dissolving of your relationship. But at the very least, it does mean that the dynamic of the relationship has shifted.

What Lies Ahead?

Now the crossdresser is faced with the very real prospect of what comes next. Whether as a lifelong crossdresser or as a man who discovers feminine dressing as an adult, there are choices.

You can continue to live a partially fulfilled life where the two sides of the same mind never meet beyond the shadows of solitude and secrecy. You can wait to be discovered and suffer the consequences, hoping for the best while assuming the worst. Or you can share your burden with your partner, with the hopes that understanding, support and love will rule the day.

I am not advocating that you reveal yourself to your partner, dear crossdresser. That is a decision that must be weighed heavily by you. I do not know enough about you or your partner to begin to understand your situation and what has led you up to this moment of contemplation.

Remember Galileo?

He theorized that the world was not the center of the universe, but instead that it traveled around the sun. By speaking out his truth about cosmic mechanics, he was condemned and placed under a lifetime house arrest by the Roman Catholic Church. His words were heresy and he was admonished for them.

He knew the risks of letting his views come out. He faced those risks and lived out the rest of his life with those consequences. He lived with the truth, as he understood it.

I know I am over simplifying the processes and boiling down what the possible outcomes are. But sometimes placing a single *KISS* on the forehead of the issue – Keep It Simple, Silly – is the best course of action. And, maybe, my own story will help you and your partner find some enlightenment and hope.

At the end of the day, all we have is our hope, positivity, empathy, and the capacity for love. The rest are only things we have or want to have. And, sometimes, what we have now is far better than we realize.

We don't always get what we want, as Mick Jagger sang, but consider this… there are people out there who will never have what you have right now.

Truth And Consequences

Acceptance of what has happened is the first step to overcoming the consequences of any misfortune.
~ William James

Men who are in earnest are not afraid of consequences.
~ Marcus Garvey

Self Examination

Socrates wrote, "The unexamined life is not worth living."

And his words should ring so very true too for all people, not just for crossdresssers. We should always take a moment to reflect on who we are and where we are going on our life's journey. And we should not do it only once, but periodically. It is a truth that can be summed up by the following example.

I read J.D *Salinger's The Catcher in the Rye* many years ago when I was a young man with the entire world in front of me. The novel's protagonist Holden Caulfield was considered a rock star of teenage rebellion. I rallied behind his cause, completely identifying with his teenage angst and his rage against the machine. I reread the novel much more recently, as many of us have done, and found Caulfield to be a whiney punk who needs to grow up and get a job! And did you know that there is a crossdresser in the book?

As we gain experiences in life, our opinions subtly change. We mature, for better or worse, becoming more positive or maybe more cynical. We get set in our ways... you can't teach an old dog new tricks, they say... and many other sayings about getting old that I can't remember. Heck, I'm still trying to figure out why I have a cup holder that slides out on my computer tower. Hmmmm

Ignorance Is No Excuse

Type in the following quote on Google, *There are no experts, only varying degrees of ignorance*, and you will find many who have used it to illustrate whatever point they were making. The same quote can apply to crossdressers and their partners.

It is a universal truth.

In fact, what is truth?

What follows are my truths as my little primitive brain understands them. Get ready for a bulleted list!

- Sylvester Stallone said, "You're the disease, and I'm the cure!" Ah, movie quotes. I love them! I don't believe there is a cure for crossdressing. Medical science will not be able to shock it out of us. The Church will not be able to dissuade us with threats of eternal damnation, a litany of prayers to a higher power, or an exorcism.
- I believe it is easier for someone to accept learning about a crossdresser when it doesn't affect him or her on a personal level. "*Hey, my cousin is a crossdresser! It's cool.*", is fine, but wait you are saying that about your boyfriend or husband. That tends to be a different story. Then it becomes a 24/7 situation instead of an anecdotal one. Ironically, people are more apt to become champions

Living with Crossdressing: Defining a New Normal

- or advocates for members of the transgender community when it does affect them on a personal level.
- People confuse the following terms: transgender versus transsexual versus transvestites.
  I know I confuse them. Yes, I consider crossdressers to be part of the transgender category as I take the term of transgender as "across gender". Crossdresser a synonym for a transvestite, but they do not necessarily fall into the transsexual category. It is important to research each term and how they are defined.
- The word transvestite carries with it a heavily weighted negative connotation. Stigma drips off of the word based on decades of misconceptions, misuse, misunderstanding, and taboo.

There are many other truths, which I hope I can bring to light throughout this book, dear reader. I can only urge you to read on.

While I personally identify as a crossdresser, I cannot advocate for all people who say that they are crossdressers.

Wait! What? Why are you writing this book, then?

Let me rephrase that for you. I know who I am, but I cannot know the history, desires, and experiences of anyone who is reading this book. Are you just a crossdresser (still hate the "just" part) or looking for more? Are you into the fetish of gender bending? Are you denying that there is a real woman screaming to emerge, whose voice will only be silenced by some measure of medical gender transitioning?

I am only here to help eliminate the misconceptions, taboos, and stigmas of what crossdressers are assumed to be. Ignorance is bliss, but that type of bliss has no place here.

A Secret Shared Is A Secret Halved

Or is it?

Walter Scott wrote, "Oh, what a wicked web we weave when first we practice to deceive." His words resound with the irony of how lies complicated life, even if the lie or omission was intended to make life easier for one or all parties involved. There are many components and layers of deceit to keeping or sharing a secret.

For crossdressers, the first component is the shame and heavy emotion of keeping the secret, of keeping that one thing hidden from those we love. Fear and experience are usually the major factors as to why we continue to hold the truth so close. But it is not just one lie, is it? The Big Lie is buttressed up by a series of interconnecting Little Lies, each compounding on top of the other. Each Little Lie is validated by the fact that it is necessary to keep the integrity of the Big Lie.

For the crossdresser, there are hidey-holes throughout the attic, car trunk, closet or garage with all of their femme stuff. There are clandestine meetings in bars, cars, hotels, and houses where the crossdresser feels safe to express their femininity – alone or with others. It is an existence worthy of Cold War spy games. The secret becomes all encompassing.

There could be a discovery that forces the secret out or a trauma that makes the secret too volatile to keep. Can those you love weather the impending storm of the truth? Can they rally behind your truth? I cannot answer that because every situation is so unique that to offer precise advice could have plenty of blowback for all involved.

Weight Of The World

So now your partner knows, however the secret comes to light.

And by the goddesses, dear crossdressers, I hope your secret was revealed with humility, a bare soul, and a hope for understanding – with no defensiveness or the casting of blame to others beyond yourself. Don't be ashamed of who you are, but do take responsibility for keeping the secret.

You feel better, right?

Wow! Your secret is now revealed and that albatross is no longer around your neck. Where did that weight go? It didn't dissipate into thin air, I assure you. That weight lifted off you is now a crushing weight on your partner's shoulders. Are they strong enough to carry the burden?

That will all depend on the core strength of the individual. We aren't talking about Pilates here. Strength of mind, heart, character and spirit are critical to the success of any obstacle of this magnitude. You, dear crossdresser, have to help your partner carry the weight. Just because you dropped the weight of the secret on her, you are still fully responsible for picking it back up and off her frame. You must allow for your partner to build up her strength through your love and understanding, as well as her pursuit of knowledge and education (and her love for you).

Please realize that your partner is now forced to carry the weight of your secret... and has to lie about it to others. Your significant other may appear sullen and depressed, with no way to express the real reasons to friends and family who express concern about her new mood.

All partners should have the right to share the secret with someone outside the relationship. Their only course of dialogue cannot just be with the one who revealed the secret to them. There are already trust issues there, so any honest discussion may still be laced with the worry of falsehood.

I told Jen that she has every right to share my secret – now our secret – with anyone she deemed worthy. She didn't and doesn't need to get my approval to do so. I am comfortable and confident enough in my own skin to weather any questions or judgment from anyone outside of Jen and my relationship. In the end, defending *me* is not about defense, but about education. People will always judge crossdressers. It is human nature to make judgment on something that is foreign, misunderstood or different.

How do you have such confidence?

It's all an act, I assure you.

Kidding.

People don't seem to realize that it takes strength of character to admit that we are different and unique from the social norm. It also take strength to share who we truly are with those we love, putting into jeopardy the lives we have created under what some may consider false pretenses. I may be an upper middle-class white male, but I am still in this strange ethereal minority. Once we accept ourselves fully, it becomes easier to emote that confidence to others. If you are positive and upbeat, that will shine through regardless of what you are wearing.

Savannah's Story

A man's face is his autobiography. A woman's face is her work of fiction.

~ Oscar Wilde

I'm writing an unauthorized autobiography.

~ Steven Wright

Once Upon A Time

It seems most appropriate to write about my life as if it were a fairy tale. I mean there is a beautiful (ahem) princess trapped in a castle that, even if she is rescued or escapes, faces the wrath of most of the villagers and royalty of the kingdom. Are there dragons? Only if you count *drag*-ons! Is there a knight in shining armor? In fact, there are several who rescued Savannah from the evils that men (and women) do. It is a tale that spans the ages and across hundreds of miles. Riveting adventures from childhood to adulthood, filled with self-discovery and enlightenment.

Oh, enough!

Maybe I should have the Star Wars *Long, long ago, in a galaxy far away...* scroll to give you all the backstory? Nah. That wouldn't cover what I feel I need to tell, either. My story will basically be a series of vignettes, hopefully illustrating my journey to date and my hopes for the future.

"I was born a poor black child. I remember the days, sittin' on the porch with my family..." Wait. That was Steve Martin's Navin R. Johnson character from the 1979 movie, *The Jerk*.

Here Goes Everything

Anyway, my childhood upbringing was nothing special or extraordinary, except to say that it was extraordinary in its ordinariness. I was born in 1971 in Detroit, Michigan to blue-collar lower middle class parents, with a sister two years older, and eventually a little brother born four years after me. Yes, I was the middle child – the forgotten child – who typically disappears from the family dynamic.

I was quiet, introverted, and sometimes shy. I ran, played, and enjoyed suburban life with the other kids on the close-knit dead end block. Back then, we were able to play out in the streets or in the neighbors' yards from sun up to sundown during the summer, with only the fear that you better be home when the street lights came on or when a parent called out your name for dinner from the side screen door.

I never imagined that my life was anything outside the normal. What would I know? I was just a little kid. Except there came that one fateful day where my curiosity about those clothes I saw my mother fold and put away got the better of me. I don't rightly recall the exact age or date but I would put the first quest at roughly age five. Why did her white bras fascinate me? Was it the shimmer of the material or the hints of lace? To this day, I cannot recall why I originally wanted to touch her clothing or wanted to try them on. I don't know why I wanted to wad up face towels or socks to fill out the cups so that the shape was more like my mom. I continued to sneak a peek at my mom's clothes as often as it was safe to do so.

It just felt right.

What did not feel right was the fact that I knew I was being bad. Not because of the act of dressing in my mom's bra and girdle, and sometimes those black patent two inch heels that I never saw her wear, but because I knew I was trespassing into other people's belongings.

Don't touch your sister's toys. Don't go into our room.

I understood the concept of privacy and personal space. My dad had (and still has) several rifles that he stored under his bed and in his closet. I really had no interest in handling the weapons. There is an inherent draw to the power of a gun for a young boy but I had enough fear and respect for them to know to leave them alone.

Interestingly enough, while I knew it was wrong to sneak into my parents' room – and eventually, my sister's room – to find feminine clothing to try on, I never felt that the act of dressing was wrong. It seemed natural. But I inherently knew that I was doing something that my parents wouldn't appreciate if they found out. Between the two, I think I was more worried about the consequence of the trespassing than getting caught crossdressing.

Growing Pains

This process went on for several years, from pre-adolescence through my teenage years. And, as I wrote earlier, the teenage years brought with them teenage hormones and a progression from secret dressing for a sense of comfort to secret dressing that was more for visual fantasy and self-exploration. I loved to see myself in the mirror and wonder what it would feel like to be a girl. What did they feel?

Living with Crossdressing: Defining a New Normal

You know the old saying?

If I had boobs, I would be playing with them all day long!

And that is aptly put to explain how it felt. I wished I had breasts that would fill out the bra I was wearing. *Why?* Because stuffing the bra with socks or face towels seemed like a cheat. And it didn't do anything to get me closer to understanding my feminine side. Sure, I vaguely saw something in the mirror that was somewhat feminine (if I squinted long enough) but there was a divide that I knew in my heart I would never be able to realize.

Sears Roebuck used to have a powerhouse direct mail catalog where you could buy almost anything – from clothing and tools to pre-fabricated houses! I used to look at the pictures of the women in their bras, panties, and slips with the hopes that I could look like that one day. What I realize now is that I have a huge appreciation of the female form. It is a perfection I strive for in my feminine presentation when crossdressing.

In my early teenaged years, trying lipstick was as far into the application of makeup as I would venture. If I stared only at my lips, I could ignore the rest of my obviously masculine face. It served to make the process a little bit more complete when used in addition to whatever clothing I tried on. The teenage years brought with it my sister's pantyhose, bathing suits and leotards. That was also when I seriously started reading comics.

And who were my favorite characters? I liked Batman, Superman and the Flash, but I loved Wonder Woman and the Black Canary. And, yes, I tried to use my sister's pantyhose and black bathing suit to recreate Black Canary's look, sans boots, choker, and bolero jacket or blond hair. I knew that I could never be successful in trying to replicate Wonder Woman's look (I feel that way even now!), especially after Lynda Carter epitomized the character in such grand and visual fashion. So, even before its time as something mainstream to do, I had unknowingly had my first attempt at cosplay.

Nothing more notable occurred during those years before high school. Well, that's not necessarily true. There were two instances where I was almost caught in the act. One of the times I was caught trying to put a bikini bottom back into my sister's drawer. I realized my mom was in her bedroom seconds before I went into my sister's room with the bikini. I stuffed the bathing suit bottoms into my sock drawer but not before my mom came in and demanded to know what I was doing. I showed her the bikini bottoms and explained it away as a prank I was playing on my sister.

Did she believe you?

I thought she did. Her reaction to seeing me with my sister's bikini bottoms was the comment, "Do you want people to think you're gay?". Of course, my mom was the same one who accused me of smoking after finding damp sawdust in my winter jacket pocket (I worked with my dad on a side job). At any rate, I re-doubled my efforts to keep my activities hidden.

In high school, I did have a few girlfriends. I believe it was my senior year that I started becoming sexually active. I was lucky enough to have a girlfriend that I had been able to share about my want to wear women's clothing and underwear, and was lucky enough that she was open to encounters where one, or both of us in turn, wore lingerie. It was a turning point for my feelings of acceptance and confidence.

Getting An Education

The positive feelings did not last long. High school turned into college, with full-time jobs, school projects and a change in girlfriends. The university was a commuting college so I continued to live at home, missing out on any alone time I could have had to discover more about myself. The one girlfriend that ended up being my wife (sorry, spoiler alert!) was not receptive to the idea of my wanting to dress. Therefore, my growth into understanding my authentic self was replaced with the responsibilities of my studies at school and trying to provide for my new family. With all that being said, the feeling of wanting to dress never went away.

I was able to secure a few concessions from my wife such as periodically wearing a teddy to bed and a single romantic interlude where she agreed to let me dress. It ended up being awkward and unfulfilling. I had high expectations as to how the experience would play out and I assumed that my wife's agreement was wholehearted. My want was too much and her want was too little. Therefore, the experience fizzled and my confidence for the growth of my identity was stunted. With a reminder that my wife was not supportive of my alter identity, I began to feel that I was abnormal and wrong to feel the way I did.

Well, more life changes occurred. In the early 1990s, my wife and I began a photography and graphic design business. We succeeded in the Detroit Tri-County area for a time, but the economy – and our inexperience in marketing our business and our then-novice talent – forced us to look elsewhere for employment. The opportunities that presented themselves ended up being in a different state of the union altogether!

In 1995 we moved to the Big Apple, sharing a studio

apartment in Manhattan's upper east side for a year with my wife's brother, his girlfriend and their baby. You guessed it... not too many opportunities to dress.

We worked 9 to 5. We enjoyed the company of our family. We took advantage of the sights and sounds of the city. After a year, my wife and I had saved enough to get our own apartment in the same area. The hopes of returning to a life where I had opportunities to dress again were close at hand.

Had I been unhappy during those previous months? It's hard to recall but I remember that I did periodically think about dressing. But I knew that opportunities would be scarce so I had braced for that reality. I worked hard and focused on what I could do.

With the move to our own apartment, the hopes of dressing enfemme were realized. I bought new underwear and started to dress on a daily basis under my male clothes. I finally felt more complete again, after the twelve-month drought.

The More Things Change

Another milestone started with an unexpected conversation on a Thanksgiving family holiday road trip between Michigan and New York. My wife told me about how she and a female co-worker had been discussing their thoughts of experimentation with lesbianism.

That was shocking enough. My wife had been previously hurt by a high school boyfriend who had discovered his true sexual orientation during their relationship, and had told me several stories of being grossed out by women hitting on her.

I continued to listen. I really didn't have a choice since I was driving at the time and there weren't too many rest stops to pull into for the duration of the conversation. She continued by saying that she would allow me to freely crossdress if I agreed to allow her to pursue this experiment with her co-worker.

What a deal!

I am not saying that I was onboard with the idea of my wife going outside of our marriage. But I understood enough about my struggles with my gender identity to realize that her request included her own need for self-discovery. Plus, she had dangled a reward for my consent and I was happy to be given permission to openly pursue crossdressing past the break point I had found myself at.

The upside was that the girl that my wife became involved with also took an interest in my feminine development. She helped to pick out club wear for me. She gave me a couple pointers for comportment and how to move when dancing. Another co-worker of my wife's, an openly lesbian woman, also came to the apartment to give me my first full makeover. She and her girlfriend became instrumental in helping me be comfortable in a full feminine guise. While my wife was otherwise engaged with her new girlfriend, I had the support of these other women (my first den mothers) to support me as we went out to nightclubs in Queens and Manhattan.

It was a heady time in my life as Savannah. I was in full feminine makeup. I was out in public. I had the support of others. I was accepted and allowed to flourish. My den mothers were fearless and their confidence bled off onto me. I felt like I belonged, even though it was under the veil of the clubbing nightlife and with friends who were also not the mainstream with their own sexuality.

The Undiscovered Country

Speaking of sexuality...

During Savannah's roaring 1990s, several things occurred. I accepted who I was, I struggled with my sexual identity, and, last but not least, I discovered my name.

This was the first time I accepted that I indeed fell under the label and umbrella of the LGBTQ community as a transvestite. Back in those days, the term of crossdresser had not yet replaced the more clinical moniker. I spoke the words out loud to one of my co-workers. I was proud of who I was becoming and wanted to shout it out in proclamation to whoever I could. Yeah, I was still pretty dumb. But I was lucky enough to tell only those people that were supportive and open-minded. I also wanted to tell some of my family.

I sent a letter to my sister with a photo of me dressed as Savannah with a note to call me. Back in those days, the Internet was still a baby and I resorted to the old school snail mail method of paper, pen and film to come out to my sibling. Although she didn't understand what it all meant to be me, she and her husband were both very supportive and loving to me. I thanked them for that act of kindness. I still have their wonderful typewritten responses in a four-page letter back to me.

As a transvestite, I assumed that I must also be gay. I struggled with the fact that while I loved to be with women I thought that as a feminine dresser I was supposed to be attracted to men. Yes, I fell into the same traps of misconception as everyone else. My wife, her co-workers, and I went to a bar and restaurant called Lucky Cheng's where the staff and entertainers were all drag queens and transvestites. They were gorgeous. I found them attractive. So, again, the idea was reinforced that I must be gay (because I knew they were men underneath it all). But I wasn't attracted to any man presenting as a man.

Therefore, another discovery was made. It was okay to be attracted to a man dressed as a woman. *Why?* Because those crossdressing men represented what I still find so attractive about women. These performers had perfected the art form of feminization in their presentation, their mannerisms, speech, and all the rest. I was envious at that time because I was still a novice in my own craft. I adore femininity and the inherent power that it holds. Men hold no attraction or interest for me. It is the underlying feminine current that women possess, both in presentation and personality that holds the appeal for me.

And as a grand finale, I discovered my name. Like the genesis of any good stripper or drag name, you usually use the formula of your first pet's name plus the street you grew up on. Well, I surely wasn't going to answer to the name Shaggy.

And don't call me Shirley.

I wanted something exotic, but accessible. I wanted a name that didn't sound like a stripper moniker or used an "I" in place of a "y". And I didn't want a name that made me sound like a spinster. I didn't have any ideas. My den mothers and my wife's girlfriend threw out names but none sounded right. Then, the name came to me out of the southern blue.

Savannah was now my name, and it represented my identity as a woman. It completed me as a person, even if I still had years to go to perfect my presentation and confidence.

Times, They Are A-changing

I had discovered much about myself. I had accepted and declared in a loud voice my label of transvestite. I had given myself a feminine name. I better understood my position in life, grasping my basic gender identity and reaffirming my sexual identity.

My wife came to her own revelations that she was, indeed, a lesbian. I was shocked! I was happy for her discovery, but I knew that I couldn't exist in a loveless marriage. It would be a sham. I didn't want only the guise of intimacy, but the real thing. I felt I deserved that. And I felt that it would break my heart if I continued in the relationship with the assumption that I would see her with other partners. So we divorced.

That decision was not the price to be paid. That action was for the best for both of us. We could both move on with our own pursuits of happiness. I moved to Queens, New York, to be closer to my job and to cut the cost of rent. I became involved with another woman, hopeful that her knowledge of my feminine self would allow the creation of a more balanced relationship.

And it was good. She was fine with my dressing. She went out to the same clubs I was familiar with and we enjoyed each other's company. All seemed to be becoming more normal and accepted.

At that time, another of my female co-workers told me she had a boyfriend who dressed. We made a plan to go to a club on Steinway Street in Astoria. I knew what drag queens were and some of the other fetish factions that exists, but my co-worker's boyfriend was a crossdressing type that I had not encountered before.

When they came over to our apartment I met them in the

lobby, fully dressed. The woman looked ready for the club but the boyfriend was still in boy mode. We went upstairs. He did change into a LBD (little black dress), hose, and heels... and that was it.

I was confused.

No makeup, no jewelry, no wig.

I tried to wrap my brain around it anyway. If that was his preference, who was I to say it was wrong? Heck, I was dressed in my own LBD and fully decked out en femme. Who was I to judge?

We clubbed for a bit and had a good time. Then the boyfriend did something else that confused me. After a couple hours, he went to the bathroom and returned with his boy clothes on. Why would he go through the effort to dress and shed out of it after a couple of hours? It was a wig scratcher, for sure. The thought has stuck with me, even if I didn't understand what it meant.

On another topic of discovery, I now realize that my girlfriend may have been worldlier and more in tune then I was. There had been an evening where I had been particularly stressed at work that day. She told me that maybe dressing would make me feel better. She was right. The feel of the material through my fingers and the way the clothing caressed my body did make me calmer and more relaxed. It did take some time for the stress to bleed off after dressing, but spending the evening dressed did allow me to focus on something other than work.

So all was right with the world. My girlfriend was supportive. I was discovering my balance between my male and female personas, and my confidence as Savannah.

But life has a way of changing without you wanting it to.

Back Down The Rabbit Hole

The relationship did not work out.

Not because of my two halves, but because of hers.

What the heck are you talking about? I thought she was a real woman?

I assure you she was (and still is) a real woman, folks. In our case, I now more fully grasp that she was struggling with her own identity. Not a crisis of gender identity, but one of racial identity. Her mother was Irish and her father was African American. Her Irish grandparents, due to a breakdown of her nuclear family dynamic, raised her. She didn't feel accepted by either race. I was still too immature and focused on my own development to understand fully what she was dealing with. And I was still too fresh off my divorce to want to be involved in such heady dilemmas.

So we both moved on.

Such is the way of love and relationships... and life.

And, hopefully, each experience impacts us enough to allow us to see the world in a different way.

Because I spent so much time at the office, I began to date another co-worker. She had what I needed. She was smart, focused, strong, and free of drama. As with my previous girlfriend, I made sure she was aware of Savannah. I sat down with her after work one day and showed her a photo of me as *her*. I wanted all the cards on the table. If she was not ready for the idea of being with a crossdresser, I would rather have loved and lost early versus later.

I was pleasantly surprised that she was okay with it. She was definitely a graduate of the old school, but being raised in NYC allowed for her to have more exposure to the concept of crossdressing. We eventually moved in together and the relationship flourished – as they typically do in the dreaded *honeymoon phase*. Why is it a phase, why can't it be for always? Anyway, I digress. I showed her all of my clothes and shoes. She even tried on several of my dresses. It was a novelty for her. It was something new and interesting.

But her and Savannah did not go out to the dance clubs, or even to dinner. That wasn't her scene. I understood that. She was a little bit older and past all that adolescent partying. She had raised two kids by herself – working fulltime – after her own divorce. I was attracted to her no-nonsense attitude.

We were together for fifteen years so I will not bore you with the minutia of each and every year. Over the years we saved up enough to buy a house, marriage was proposed (although we never married), we had several dogs running around the house, worked together in the same office, took in her daughter's family for a time, and lived life.

During those years, after the novelty of my crossdressing seemed to wear off I started to feel that she was becoming more disapproving of my female side. I only dressed at home on occasion. Each time I did dress up (no makeup, no wig), her reactions evolved from a sideways glance and disinterest to an eventual eye roll.

To let you in on a little secret, I am a very sensitive individual. I take things personally. I am fairly empathic and can feel how you feel. Where my empathy has a chink in its armor is when it misreads the reasons behind those reactions. I am a bit more enlightened now, but in those days it was a continuing reminder that I had lost the support I had once enjoyed.

The Great Pumpkin

One glaring example I recall of her disapproval occurred one weekend during Halloween.

Yep,

Halloween.

We shared a co-op in a community in Northern New Jersey. The property had a lake, a couple of pools, and a community center. There was an event on the calendar for a costume party. We had been together for seven years at that point, if memory serves.

I was excited to dress as a China girl, buying the dress, the sandals, and the straight jet-black wig with bangs. Although she was aware that I had made this plan, she became more and more distant about it. I tried to ignore her bad vibes and enjoy preparing for the evening. When I was ready to leave for the other side of the lake, she told me she didn't want to show up with me to the party.

I was devastated.

I was close to just taking everything off and forgetting the whole event, but decided to soldier on without her support. I went to the party a little bit early (because I am a stickler for promptness, plus wanted to get away from the bad energy at home) and waited for my friends to arrive. I helped one of them out of her car (because she had a cane and leg cast) and was delighted that she didn't recognize me. I was also delighted that, when she did realize it was me under the wig, she was totally cool with it.

The other women seemed to enjoy my costume, as well. Maybe because they thought it was brave that a man would attempt the costume and show a feminine side (because their husbands wouldn't dare to try it). Maybe they thought I looked convincing. Maybe it was because they liked me as a person, in general.

The men were a different story.

Their reactions fell into three camps. The first would be the typical good-natured masculine razing after seeing another man in drag. They played it off as parody and didn't act any different around me beyond the teasing. The second reaction was something more of avoidance. They were unsure how to take me, whether due to a homophobic issue or a subconscious vague attraction or appreciation they couldn't rationalize. They would wander away if I added myself to their group, even if their friends and spouses were having a good time chatting. And then there was the reaction that drinking men don't like to remember the next day. There was one man, in particular, who throughout the night would put his arm around me or pat me on my ass. He would lean in close, invading my personal space, and tell me a slurred and unintelligible secret truth or desire. The more drinks he consumed, the more pretty he promised I was.

The night was a bag of mixed reactions, from total acceptance to disdain to desire. I was amazed by the appreciation, saddened by the social awkwardness, and tickled by that one man's beer-goggled flirting.

What happened to your girlfriend? Did she show up?

Yes. About an hour into the full swing of music and dancing and socializing, she did arrive. I was happy she had made it (because I was worried about her). But she didn't want to really be near me or act as my girlfriend around me. What I know now, that I had ignored then, was the following; that she was struggling *with* being with me as a couple in public, and that she was worried *for* me because she didn't want people to start whispering about the type of person I was.

We didn't really talk about it afterward.

We should have talked about it.

There was no synergy between us as it came to understanding Savannah in our relationship. And that was the first of many situations where her reaction to me continued to weigh on my mind. If she was unable to accept me, then I was likely more a freak than I realized. How could I be confident and feel acceptance if the one person I assumed loved me the most was unable to see past the taboo and fetish that she believed my crossdressing represented?

From Mind Closet To Coat Closet

As few as six years ago (as of this original publication), I realized that I needed something more for Savannah. The chain keeping her immobile and miserable in the closet at home was becoming unbearable. A vague form of despair was eroding my normally upbeat and positive nature. Maybe my positivity and my hope for humanity were the only things that allowed me to continue for as long as I had.

I was afraid of who I was. Savannah was something to be ashamed of. My partner had rejected me so why should I continue to believe that I was a normal person? But then I found a measure of courage to make an appointment with a woman named Karen on Long Island at a business named Femme Fever, (my girlfriend and I were living on the island at this point) who gave me my first professional makeover.

Karen's business had a closet full of clothes and a cabinet with a variety of wigs and heels. I had brought some of my things, as well, and spent a few hours with someone who understood me and catered to me. She whipped up different looks and I explored my femininity through photography. Although I still only saw my male form in most of the photos, there were a few where the captured smile showed a comfort with my feminine side. It was a moment of bliss and re-discovery of Savannah.

For those couple hours I felt complete.

Then I returned to reality.

But my new reality wasn't the same as it was. At home, I was still in the closet and contemplating full dressing in secret, but now something had brightened within me.

I was still afraid to discuss my desires to crossdress with my girlfriend so it wasn't until a year later – when my girlfriend went out of town to visit her sister – that I returned to Karen for another makeover. More acceptance and confidence bloomed in my mind. I stopped making excuses for myself. I faced the fear of my girlfriend's disapproval and told her that I wanted to go to one of Karen's discussion groups.

I wasn't adept with my own makeup so I made the appointment with Karen to do it for me before the discussion group. I was nervous as Savannah, but interacted with the other crossdressers that were in attendance. We sat on couches and chairs in Karen's den and each of us took a turn telling our story, as we understood it. We got to hear other stories, finding out that pieces of their tales made sense to us and proved that we were not alone in the universe. I realized that I no longer suffered from terminal uniqueness.

Open 24 Hours

I became friends with several of the crossdressers in the group over the following sessions. After I became comfortable with applying my own makeup, I would get dressed at home before driving to the discussion group, but was still rushing to get there in time.

One time I forgot to get money to pay for the session. A couple of the other gurls offered to pay my way. I was very appreciative, but made it a point that I would need to go to 7-Eleven to get money to repay them. It became a running joke throughout the evening that I would soon have to face the harsh white fluorescent bars of the mini-mart.

And it happened. Two of the crossdressing girls, Victoria and Marisol, drove in a convoy with me to find a 7-Eleven close to a bar we were hoping to go to after our group session. The bar had closed down indefinitely, but the 7-Eleven had not. Victoria and I ventured from our cars to the front door. An older woman held the door for us. I told her a hushed 'thank you'. Victoria got something to drink and I withdrew $40 from the ATM. The cashiers looked at Victoria (she was wearing a plaid skirt and thigh high boots), smiling and telling us to come again.

We made our way back to the parking lot where I could repay Marisol. It was then that I realized all the fears I had let pile up over the past few years had been unrealized and unrealistic. Angry mobs didn't materialize with pitchforks and torches. I wasn't pointed out as a freak or an undesirable. I was just another person living in the world.

From that moment on I never looked back at the fear of being Savannah. My friends and I would go out to the bars, dance clubs, and out to dinners. We enjoyed the dancing and sisterhood, choosing to spend our time chatting and basking in the knowledge that we were entitled to be the people we needed to be.

Needless to say, my relationship with my girlfriend did not

work out. Some of it stemmed from my revelations concerning Savannah and what I needed out of life and from my partner. Some of it was due to a new family dynamic that I couldn't deal with. Some was just the decay of the relationship that seemed too broken to be fixed to a point of contentment.

    I had much to do with why the relationship ended. I played a big part assuming things and not communicating my needs and expectations. And I wasn't ready for the commitments that she had made on behalf of others in her life that she loved unconditionally. We continued to work together in the same office, finally able to return to a point in our relationship where there was no animosity of the past, both looking forward to our individual futures.

Our Story – Savannah & Jen

Love is composed of a single soul inhabiting two bodies.
                                                    ~ Aristotle

The best and most beautiful things in this world cannot be seen or even heard, but must be felt within the heart.
                                                    ~ Helen Keller

Fairy Tales

And they lived happily ever after.

Those are the words that all little girls want to hear at the end of the fairy tales read to them at bedtime. But in life, all people – men and women – want their own *happily ever after*. Whether for their personal lives, their careers, their families, or enlightenment of self – or a combination of some or all of the above – each of us wants to live a life filled with meaning and purpose.

For me, I yearn for a life where my male and female sides have a balance, where each is accepted and loved equally by my partner. For some crossdressing men, this ideal may be considered so unattainable that it is akin to being on the same level as locating the mythical Holy Grail.

Not Just A Costume

And this is where *my story* becomes *our story*. After the split with my girlfriend from the previous chapter, I became involved (you guessed it) with another co-worker. Hey, I can't help it if that is where I spend most of my time! And she loves AMC's The Walking Dead, so bonus points there. I had met Jen when she was hired but really didn't speak much with her during her first year. Then we started talking about TWD and argued over the merits of Rick Grimes, the main character. Flash-forward to us spending time together after her attendance at an event I was part of and we come to the point where we both realized that our relationship was reaching that next level of intimacy.

Continuing with the same formula that I employed with all of my girlfriends throughout my adult life, I felt it was important to reveal my authentic self to her. I showed her a picture from my smart phone (yes, I had graduated into the digital age when showing photos of Savannah). Jen had seen me dressed in my superhero cosplay costumes at the office Halloween parties. She said, "So? I've seen your Halloween costumes before." I had to explain that it wasn't just a costume and that dressing as a woman was part of who I was.

It was a sobering moment and a shocking revelation to Jen. How should she respond to being told that crossdressing was part of the everyday life of the man she was interested in? What were the basis questions to ask me?

- How long have you been doing it?
- So does that mean you like men?
- Do you go out in public?

- How often do you dress?
- Do you want to be a woman?

All were valid questions to have asked, especially from a novice with limited understanding and experience with our kind. Instead, I relayed to her a short-form of my story, preempting her questions by answering them before she could think to ask them. I have included an essay in the next chapter written by Jen that tells of that evening from her perspective. It's worth the read.

Jen and I parted ways for the evening, having dropped this shocking news on her prior to having to leave for a previous commitment. But I quickly didn't feel right about my decision to leave. She was now in a fragile state and, in my absence, turned to her best friend. Coincidentally, her best friend had herself been involved with a crossdressing man. You would think that a friend who was in a relationship with a crossdressing man would have all sorts of insight.

She had insight, all right.

Jen's friend, Patty, had been involved in a very intense on/off relationship with a fetish dresser. According to her, the sex was focused on his dressing in fishnets and garters (and more). She struggled with her feelings about the intensity of the relationship and her obsessive emotions over it. Jen and Patty revealed what they knew and Patty warned her to dump me outright.

After my shortened evening out, I asked Jen if I could come back to her apartment. She relented and we found ourselves sitting on her living room couch. The space was filled with a mix of awkward silences and stilted questions from Jen that I answered as honestly as I could.

The experience was overwhelming for Jen – and for me. I

faced almost assured rejection of a woman I had come to care about. All because of who I was. And Jen faced the prospect that if she pursued the relationship she would be involved with a man who was not completely a man.

Two reasons stayed the date of my execution. The first was that she felt a strong attraction and connection to me (my male side). It was the reason that we were on the precipice of a relationship to begin with. The second reason, in her post-divorce, she realized that she wanted to try this relationship because she felt I could be *The One*.

What about the crossdressing bombshell?

Well, thank you for the compliment… wait… you meant the news I dropped on her lap? Sorry.

Jen admits that she compartmentalized her reservations about my feminine side because of the overwhelming notion that she could have possibly discovered her soulmate in me. With a bit of new relationship jitters, the undiscovered country of what a crossdressing partner would mean to her, and the promise that we could continue to be friends if all else failed, Jen ventured into the unknown with me.

Lift Up Your Hearts

That solitary adventure led to another interlude, then a third. We were left wondering how we got to this point where Jen found herself in a relationship with a man she now loved (and I adore her more… although she would say she loves me more!) with this pink elephant smack dab in the middle of her living room and taking up her closet space.

She had begun the process of processing.

Living with Crossdressing: Defining a New Normal

How does one live with a crossdresser?

What is to be expected?

Her only practical knowledge had come from a woman who had begged her to never see me again. In fact, Patty quickly ended their friendship as a consequence of Jen not heeding her advice. Jen tried to broach the subject of their struggling relationship (and about me) but was rebuffed each time a chance to discuss it was presented. Patty felt that, like her lover, I was a pervert only interested in kinky sex and wearing lingerie to get off. Hey, I enjoy my sensuality and sexuality as much as the next crossdresser – maybe more so – but that doesn't mean I'm a pervert!

But the true tipping point between the three of us came on a fateful day during a Sunday morning service at the church the three of us attended. Yes, I believe in God. I strive to be a good person, to do good work and to care for my fellow human. Jen and I both enjoyed many of the pastor's sermons, the fellowship, and the spirit that buzzed through us during the act of singing. Before the sermon began, the congregation was asked to stand and shake hands with those around them. As would be the case that day, Patty and her young teenage daughter were seated directly behind us.

I shook the hand of Patty's daughter. You could see in Patty's face the disgust and repulsion she felt toward me. There was a sense of profound disapproval. It was as if she expected that I was going to kidnap her daughter with the intent of molesting her. Patty truly felt that I was a perverted individual, maybe as bad as a pedophile.

It was a polarizing moment.

I understand who I am. At most times, I am in balance with my two sides. Patty, who only knew me through short greetings and by my label as a crossdresser, felt validated to lump me in as just one of thousands of kinky, sexually deviant men who got off on dressing en femme. I was just a statistic based on Patty's one personal experience.

I truly understand that assessing our personal experiences is one of the tools we use to perceive the world around us. If you touch a hot pan on a stovetop, you are less apt to make the same mistake again. You become more cautious. Unfortunately, her experience was just one sliver in the spectrum of what crossdressing means for men (as you have seen in our earlier chapters). But the damage had been done, right under God's nose in his own house.

I was hurt.

Jen was hurt and hurt for me. Patty had slandered the man she loved. After the shock of the actual event wore off, I felt pity for Patty. Her *blindered* understanding about the motivations of crossdressing men will forever keep her from an enlightened life.

For Your Consideration ~

Are all redheads of the same temperament? Do alcoholics have the same story or genetics or trauma that led them to drink? It's easy to dismiss all crossdressers as being the same, but that is a limited worldview on the topic.

Understanding a crossdresser begins with an education, not only from the crossdresser's mouth but also from as much relevant reading material and research as is available. Confiding in family, friends or a therapist to talk through their feelings about our crossdressing is understandable and should be fully supported.

Re-Education

Jen had asked me questions about my wants, likes, and origins. But at the onset, I advised her to do some reading. The most notable books I was aware of at the time were *My Husband Betty* by Helen Boyd and *My Husband Wears My Clothes* by Peggy J. Rudd. Jen, through her own research, found a short ebook entitled *An Addicted Crossdresser* and a longer effort in *Head Over Heels*. After each reading, Jen was able to ask me more intelligent questions.

But knowledge, like many things, comes with a price. Jen's reading replaced her fears based on ignorance with fears based on education. Ugh! Now, because of her reading, I had to start answering questions about transitioning to womanhood. When I told her I was happy being a part-time female, our conversation went something along these lines:

"In the book, many men wanted to transition," Jen said. "They said they were happy to just crossdress, then decided a few years later to be women!"

"I'm happy being who I am," I replied.

"That's what the men in the book said, too," she stated.

"But I like my parts the way they are," I insisted.

While Jen was discovering more about the crossdressing and transgender communities, some of her reading steered her toward several crossdressing men who ultimately made the realization that they needed to take that final step in the journey toward their female gender identity. It is difficult to argue that I am happy as a man who only wants to dress as a woman once a week when my response to the question has already been chronicled in print by a transitioned male-to-female (MtF) woman.

It's true; I had questioned my gender identity throughout the years. I still fantasize about waking up one day and looking in the bathroom mirror to see a beautiful buxom curvy woman staring back at me. But that same fantasy allows me the ability to morph back into my male biology anytime I chose.

I want it to be easy.

I am totally lazy.

That's a fact I am okay with sharing.

The fantasies are about being able to present as a female without all the crossdressing trappings of body shapers, breast forms, hip pads and shaving. All that preparation is sometimes exhausting. There are times where the thought of transforming into Savannah after ten hours of work is daunting and off-putting. The sixty to ninety minutes it takes me to transform can be therapeutic or it can be drudgery.

So Jen continued to read and ask me questions that I answered to the best to my ability. But fears are sometimes irrational and all consuming. Before we lived together (another spoiler!), I was excited to show her all of Savannah's stuff. Jen came over to my apartment and I started parading out all my dresses, heels, and my wigs on their individual wig stands. Her face went waxen and slack, her eyes went wide.

Jen was overwhelmed by the sheer immensity of the display. She hadn't realized that I had more women's stuff than men's stuff. She felt I must want to be a woman more often than a man because of the amount of female gear I had.

My excitement was quickly replaced with a feeling of rejection. I took her shock at the amount of clothing in my closet as not accepting the feminine part of me.

For Jen it was too much, too quickly.

I could see on her face that she was uncomfortable and I stopped showing her my things. We talked about how she was feeling. She shared her emotions and I was forced to look at myself in plainer terms. I had to realize that this was all new to her. Jen had to tell me several times that '… you have had a lifetime to understand who you are, while I'm still trying to figure this out. You are expecting me to process all this in days'.

It continues to be difficult for me to accept that even if someone loves me unconditionally as a man, there can still be conditions in the fine print when it comes to finding out your man also wants to present as a woman.

The Unveiling

Soon thereafter we made plans for her to see me as Savannah in the flesh. For the first time in my life, I had a woman that wanted to see the transformation from start to finish. She didn't want a repeat of the closet reveal. She didn't want to be overwhelmed or shocked into submission by my sudden change into femininity. So she looked on as a spectacular to my ritual of becoming female. From putting on all of my undergarments and padding, to watching me apply my foundation and makeup, to helping me zip up my dress, to the final reveal with my favorite red-haired wig, Jen was there for it all.

Like her, I am also not a fan of being dressed en femme halfway. I wear women's underwear every day, but to wear more without trying to present as feminine is always a little awkward for me. I look odd in the mirror. It must also look strange to Jen.

At that point, it just looks like I am a man in a dress.

And I don't want to look like a man in a dress.

I want to be passable. I want to blend in. I want people on the street to completely ignore me because they don't have a reason to give me a second glance. Or if they do give me a second glance, it's because they are trying really hard to figure out if I am a woman or a man. Passibility (for me, anyway) is an important part of the process. It may seem shallow, but I see it as perfecting my craft.

Jen, at this point, had seen my femme closet and now had witnessed first hand a full-fledged transformation into Savannah.

And you know what?

She wasn't scared away.

We talked as long as we could on the subject that night in my bedroom (without it becoming too much to process again). She didn't think I was a weirdo (well, maybe she did a little), letting me know that she didn't recognize me and complimenting me that I looked pretty.

What else could a crossdresser want to hear from their partner? Jen had embraced the notion that I could be a serious crossdresser and not be an embarrassment. She saw Savannah, even if she couldn't find the male *me* under the makeup and hair. My dressing for Jen for the first time was a rousing success – for both of us.

At this point, Savannah was not going out very often with her gurlfriends. In fact, I did not go out at all in those first few months, either alone or with Jen. But the end of the year was looming and one of my major favorite events was on the horizon.

Living with Crossdressing: Defining a New Normal

Costumes And The Comic Con

I am a huge comic book, sci-fi and zombie nerd. I'm proud to admit it. And the eastern seaboard Mecca for nerds, like me, is the New York Comic Con in Manhattan every October. Jen was excited to be a part of the experience (and was interested in cosplay). I would be able to show Jen the ropes of going to the annual New York Comic Con and involve her with another passion that was close to my heart. We spent several weeks finding an extra ticket and assembling our costumes. And then the big weekend arrived.

The comic book convention, like crossdressing, covers many more genres than just comic books. It is a sensory overload of comics, pop culture, movies and television, manga, sci-fi, and cosplay! Jen kept pace throughout the event schedule over the first three days like a champ. Early Sunday morning – our cosplay day – we dressed, primped and turned into our superhero alter egos and set off for the Long Island Railroad to make our way into the city.

Jen was very nervous. She was nervous for going out in public in New York City dressed as a slinky superheroine in a skin-tight black bodysuit and shockingly white long wig. She was also nervous for me. She worried about what people would say about me, who I was dressed as, and how they would pass judgment on me. Once we arrived at the venue and started to see so many other people in costumes of all types, she relaxed and came to the realization that we were just another of hundreds of costumers in attendance.

We blended in.

People stopped us with the hopes of taking our pictures.

The day's scheduled events went without a hitch. We stood in line for the sessions I was hoping to see and Jen was supportive and engaged with the spectacle that is NYCC. We met up with a co-worker who had come to the convention with his brother. He was surprised by the both of us, but seemed to take it all in stride. He took pictures of Jen and me, even making us kiss.

I was over the moon!

I am a very tactile and affectionate boyfriend. I like to kiss, hug and touch Jen as often as I can. Some of it may stem from insecurity and some from wanting to re-enforce my love for my partner. Some of it is because I love the physical connection. And some of it is because Jen is just so gosh darn attractive!

Why are you telling us this, Savannah?

I am telling you about this part of my personality because the Comic Con demonstrated one of the divides that Jen and I face as a gurl/girl couple. Because I am so physically passionate, it is very, very difficult for me to separate or compartmentalize my feelings for my girlfriend while I am dressed en femme. I still have the same feelings toward her while she is forced to look at a completely different person than the one she fell in love with.

It is not to say that Jen loves me any less when I am dressed as Savannah. She was willing to dress up in costume in support of me (and to have the experience). She was willing to be seen in public with me at a convention that boasts tens of thousands of visitors each year giving testament enough of her commitment to us. Even now, Jen continues to work toward her own balance of what a Savannah/Jen relationship looks like. She has held my hand and put her hand on my leg (and mine on hers), but a higher degree of intimacy will probably always be a work in progress.

Or maybe never realized at all.

It's all about balance. It's all about honest communication. It's all about each partner trying to understand the other's perspective, not just trying to force his/her own beliefs on the other. There was a sense of empowerment within us as we walked the New York City streets as powerful female superheroes. There was also disappointment with the new understanding that Jen didn't *see* me (or love me?) as her life partner while dressed. And there was the realization that we still had a long way to go in our development if Savannah and Jen were ever to become a *normal* couple.

Cinderella At The Ball

There is a private annual gala event each spring on Long Island hosted by Femme Fever for crossdressers, transgender individuals, their partners and admirers. Years before, after mustering enough courage to tell my previous girlfriend that I was intending to go, the event had been cancelled and had gone on hiatus for several seasons.

But now it was back on, like Donkey Kong!

Jen and I ordered custom dresses for the gala ball. Since it was a long awaited event for me, I ordered a sparkly dress with a flowing train and black opera gloves. I was excited and ready to go. This moment was years in the making and I was filled with anticipation of the event and the joy of sharing it with Jen. We booked a hotel room at the venue and planned to make a whole weekend out of it.

The gala was on a Saturday so we arrived Friday night. After settling in, there were vague plans to meet up with some of the other gurls. I dressed as Savannah and we headed down to the lounge. I was in my element and happy.

Without even a second thought, while we were heading toward

the front desk to ask about another blanket for the room, I reached out to hold Jen's hand. She quickly pulled her hand away. For me it was instinctual and natural. To Jen, it was a moment of sheer panic, something she was totally unprepared for.

I was devastated.

After putting in the request for the blanket, we went to the bar. No one was there to meet up with. Additional disappointment took hold of me and took us back to our room. I quickly changed back into my boy clothes, taking off my wig and wiping off my makeup. It didn't seem worth it anymore to dress. The woman I love had rejected me.

That's a bit melodramatic, isn't it? Sounds like you were being a diva and a drama queen.

You are right, of course, dear reader. I was overreacting. Just because she wasn't ready to hold my hand in public didn't constitute a wholesale rejection of me (or my crossdressing). It represented the struggles she was working through. In a very selfish way, I had ignored so many obvious points. She was still coming to terms with understanding my dressing, was still worried about what other *normal* people might think about me (and us as a couple), and was dealing with the fact that a strange woman – not her boyfriend – was trying to hold her hand.

After I dressed down in the room, she asked why I had done so. She said that we still could have gone out for a walk or a drive or something. In spite of all of her fears and worries, she was still willing to support Savannah in some way. That simple act should have been enough.

But we gurls sometimes cannot see what we have. I was grateful that Jen had agreed to come with me to the ball. That was a heartfelt and heartwarming gesture. I wanted to show her my love and appreciation. Unfortunately, I found myself in a strange place. I was with the woman I love, but was forced to treat her like just a friend. I had to consciously remember that she was off limits in a more intimate way. So while I was wrestling with the idea of unrequited affection, Jen was struggling with the notion of being on a date with a beautiful feminine stranger (yeah, I said it... beautiful).

After some tears and discussions, we turned in and woke up fresh that next Saturday morning. As boyfriend and girlfriend, we checked out a local beachfront park and took in each other's company, the sun's rays, and a bit of food for the early part of the day. Eventually, we headed back to the hotel to get ready for the ball. We put on our gowns and headed down to the ballroom with our tickets.

We met up with my other gurlfriends, picked out a table, took pictures, and paraded around like silly prom dates. I quickly learned a few things, realizing that a dress train is a pain in the ass, that real women are way more comfortable without their heels, and that the gala ball was akin to fulfilling a fantasy for some gurls who do not have other outlets or opportunities to express themselves.

The event brought out all types. Well, not all types but several types that Jen had not seen in person before that night. Aside from the normal rabble of men in ball gowns and cocktail dresses there were over-the-top drag queens, some shiny body-suited babes, and even an older gurl in a way-too-skimpy red stretch tube dress.

One of Jen's fears was coming to fruition. Even though I had given her the seminar on some of the types of crossdressers across the transgender spectrum, Jen had purposefully put those other types out of her head. She had a fear that if she acknowledged

Living with Crossdressing: Defining a New Normal

those types of crossdressers it would mean that I fell into or would fall into one of those other fringe categories. She was trying to build a world where my crossdressing was to be accepted as the new normal in her life. To see so many other types of crossdressers and their intimate interaction served to overwhelm and put cracks into the veneer she had constructed for herself.

I could only counter by reminding her that some of these women had no other outlet for their femininity. Some were still discovering their sexual preferences and their gender identity. Jen was witnessing firsthand hundreds of people in their own degree of feminine expression.

The event went well, but it was all sensory overload for Jen. She went back to the hotel room and turned in after the lights came up in the ballroom. I opted to stay out with my gurlfriends for as long as I thought I could, just enjoying the freedom of being Savannah for a night.

As boyfriend and girlfriend, the next morning we ate a hearty breakfast at the local diner across from the hotel. We discussed what we had seen and heard during the weekend. Afterward, we made our way home to unpack and decompress. It was our opportunity to absorb everything that had occurred.

Fears And Flash-forwards

Since that time, Savannah and Jen attended a second Spring Gala Ball in which we were much more comfortable in our skins. We have had GNOs (girls' night out) with my other gurlfriends, dressed again (and again) for the New York Comic Con, and attended themed private parties on a monthly basis. She doesn't come with me all of the time, either due to scheduling conflicts, the fact that the venue may not be her thing (loud bars are not really conducive to chatting), or just to acknowledge that a man needs his gurl time.

We have grown in our understanding and appreciation of each other's perspective and opinions. But, of course, we continue to have fears about the present and the future. Some of those fears may be rationalized away. Some may dissipate with the passage of time. Some may haunt us for the rest of our lives.

My greatest fear is that Jen will discover that dealing with Savannah is too much of a hardship. I worry that she will feel that she could find another partner like me who does not have the additional baggage of Savannah in tow. I understand that I do take up a lot of closet space!

My other big fear is that Jen will never be able to see *me* under the makeup and finery. I love it when she says I am the prettiest girl in the room because it means that I am passable as a woman and that I don't look like my male self. But by that same notion, the fact that she can't see *me* may keep her from ever being comfortable enough to treat Savannah as the man she loves.

Jen has her own set of issues and fears. From battling the status quo and standards of normalcy, to fearing the harsh judgments, ignorance, and scorn of others, to wrestling with her own psychological limitations of acceptance and how far those lines can be blurred or pushed. She has plenty of angst to go around.

What is normal? Socially accepted behaviors change based on a person's upbringing, experiences, generational constructs, and culture. There is a fundamental difference in the acceptance of crossdressing between people born in Japan versus the United States. Where crossdressing has been part of the fabric of the culture in Asia, the same practice here in the States is more foreign an idea. And while crossplay is celebrated in other parts of the world, red-blooded Americans still have trouble rationalizing why a man would want to dress in feminine attire at all.

These factors create an environment ripe for judgment and to be seen as fetish or counter-culture. How is a woman who is in a relationship with a crossdressing male supposed to explain – or even defend – to friends and family her boyfriend's preferences? Especially when the behavior is something that maybe she can't fully understand. Even if she had a rational and logical argument to help champion her partner against all comers' judgment, the ability to sway hearts and minds is a daunting task.

Jen doesn't want me to suffer at the hands of others' disapproval. She worries about a relationship where I may be unwanted at family events because of who – or what – I am. She doesn't want me to be excluded due to an unwarranted or unplanned discovery. Jen, I think, worries more about the mobs with torches and pitchforks than I do. Some of it is fear and assumptions about people's worst nature. And we have stood witness to how people can treat each other based on hatred, ignorance, and disdain.

As Jen continues to support Savannah's right to exist, and comes to terms with Savannah as part of the fabric of her life, the new dynamic becomes the new normal. That is not to say that exposure breeds acceptance. Exposure may only result in tolerance. It is an open mind and the understanding that the man she loves still exists under the foundation; that the man she loves is actually a result of the man and the woman he is. Isn't that interesting? The man she fell in love with – the qualities that makes me who I am – is due directly to the woman I am.

But how can she love Savannah? Doesn't that make her a

lesbian? Won't she be judged if she is out in public showing affection to you?

On this point, I have to admit I have no good answers. I would love Jen to treat Savannah exactly the same as she does when I am in my male form. I see her angst as a result of years of conforming to labels created around her. But Jen has every right to her feelings of discomfort if she detects that others may be staring at her (and us). I guess the question is whether one wants to live a conformed life based on the expectations of others or live a life where each moment is a new adventure.

Jen hopes to break through the fears that have shaped her. It calls for a high level of self-esteem. It calls for a strength that allows her to not care about outside opinions, if those opinions are derogatory to the life she hopes to live for herself and me.

Heck, there were even mental blocks for Jen to use the 'proper' pronouns when together with others. It is not an easy thing to switch her brain to speak of me as a *she* and *her* versus a *he* and *him*. How do you rationalize telling a story about something we have done together as man and woman using the *her* pronoun simply because I am sitting in the booth next to her wearing a dress? It's not easy. But she puts in an extreme effort anyway because she knows it's important to me.

Jen is also becoming more comfortable uttering the word *crossdresser* in conversation when we are out in public. One time, we were in Kohl's when she pointed at a dress and mentioned that she had noticed that other crossdressers wore similar styles. I instinctively looked around to make sure we were out of earshot from the other customers.

Jen is amazing. We now shop together for dresses for her and Savannah. She has no problem trying on something for me to get me an idea of how the dress could look on me. We have even bought two of the same dress and wore them to a private event. Who wore it best? It certainly wasn't me!

In our time together, Jen and I have both grown into more enlightened individuals. I have become more introspective and conscious of who I am and why I react to things the way I do. I am trying to channel my over-sensitivity and my own fears in a more positive manner. I am trying to better understand why Jen reacts the way she does. It is about metaphysically walking in her shoes to the point where I can be more objective about who I am through her eyes.

And That's The Way It Is

Jen and I purposefully strive to understand our place in the world and our place with each other. We work to grow in understanding and acceptance. The journey is ongoing. To stop learning is to stop living. More answers should always lead to more questions.

The non-transitioning, non-fetish crossdresser may continue to be one of the last great gender identity unknowns. Will it ever be normal in mainstream society? In my case, I just want to live a positive life with Jen at my side where she appreciates and loves both my male and female sides in equal measure, where she sees changing from my male side into Savannah as nothing more than changing into a sweater on a brisk autumn day.

Jen, In Her Own Words

The real voyage of discovery consists not of seeking new landscapes, but in having new eyes.

~ Marcel Proust

Ignorance is never better than knowledge.

~ Enrico Fermi

Another Perspective

I have worked with Jen to tell the story of our lives together. I cannot claim that I transcribed all of the nuances correctly on her behalf so, in an effort to lift up and celebrate her voice, I am adding Jen's own words in this chapter. It's important to understand that our perception of events is not necessarily the perception of those around us. We color our understanding with our past experiences and blush it with our own bias.

When I read Jen's perspective for the first time, I was very emotional. Her story, in her own words, is a gift. It is a gift for her to share her struggles, her enlightenment, and her love for me. The only way I can repay her love is to continue to show her mine.

As I Recall

Savannah and I had been 'flirting' for a while. We knew each other through work. The day finally arrived where we were together outside the office. There was definitely chemistry there! We were "getting to know each other" when he pulled back and said those fateful six words that would change my world forever...

"I've got to show you something".

He sat back and started looking through his pics on his phone. He shows me one of him dressed up as a woman. I told him, "So? It's your Halloween costume." (Side note, he and a fellow male co-worker had dressed up as "hookers" and were accompanied by two women who were their male "pimps". It was cute!)

He looks at me in a deadpan way and said "No, its not...".

I looked at him.

Looked at the pic.

Looked at him.

I was rendered speechless. Literally. I seem to remember my jaw flapping up and down but no sounds would come out, or coherent thought would form. I don't remember the exact words that came from him beyond that but I remember the gist of it.

"Ask me anything."

I had nothing.

He said, "OK, the usual answers…No, I'm not gay. No, I'm not transitioning…"

I couldn't process. I leaned in for a hug and kiss. I remember him saying, "OK, I see…shut up and kiss me."

I was in shock, I suppose.

Now it needs to be pointed out here, we were not a couple at that point. We were testing the waters. But it was there. That intangible something that lets you know on some level that this is NOT your typical short-term date. That this could be The One. So without knowing it, I knew it. Our afternoon tryst was short lived because he had "an engagement" that evening. We knew going in he would be only staying for an hour or so then it was off for this mystery evening he hadn't elaborated on.

But he did fill me in on his plans now. He had an evening scheduled with the gurls. His Savannah attire was in the car, he would be changing at his friends house then out for dinner and drinks. He did not cancel this evening.

That stung.

But who was I to say differently?

He asked if he could come back after his engagement. I said probably. He left.

I was in a fog.

I called my best friend.

Patty came over right away. She could hear something was off in my voice. We sat on opposite ends of the couch and she asked me what was wrong.

I spit it out.

And burst into tears.

She let me have my cry and then begrudgingly told me the story of HER former boyfriend. He was also a cross dresser of sorts, but of the fetish variety. It was all about sex. Kinky. He tried on several occasions to drag her into his role-play. I believe she acquiesced on occasion. But it all left a bitter taste in her mouth about crossdressers in general.

She gave it a valiant attempt to persuade me to kick this guy to the curb.

I couldn't do it though! I wanted to believe that there was more to it.

Long story short, she left for the evening and I got the text that "Savannah" was done and would like to come back.

I said yes.

More conversation ensued. I tried to put it in a pocket in my brain that him being a crossdresser was ok, but struggled with it. But I couldn't just walk away from what was between us either. So my solution was to be friends.

Living with Crossdressing: Defining a New Normal

I needed time to process my feelings. Protect myself. Keep it casual.

Yeah. Didn't work. He was persistent and persuasive about wanting to make it work between us. So we carried on as a couple.

I set about the daunting task of trying to educate myself. I started reading. At that time I had a job that had a LOT of down time, and I was alone during that time. I was inhaling books.

And Savannah and I talked. He has a philosophy he lives by which is "Show, Not Tell" which served me well during this time. Slowly, a picture of a non-transitioning, crossdresser-next-door emerged. He just felt a need to express his feminine side. No more, no less.

I could live with that.

I still had to deal with the stigma associated with this new world. I had never thought of crossdressers before. Had someone mentioned the word, I immediately would envision flamboyant drag queens. The notion that there are men out there that just like to dress respectfully and have dinner or drinks together, go dancing, then go home and get back into their sweats was one that took work to wrap my brain around.

Eventually we had our first reveal, where I actually met Savannah in person. I insisted on watching the entire process. I wanted to see the evolution, not be shocked at the transformation. I didn't know it at the time, but in retrospect I could see I was actually slowly dipping my toes into this crossdressing pool. I needed baby steps to integrate the concept of Savannah into my life until it made sense.

So here was Savannah. He was very passable. Pretty. I told him so. I couldn't bring myself to think of him as a "her" yet. That would take a while. But it was nothing garish or drag queen-ish. It just...was.

It was almost anti-climatic... almost.

More processing ensued. He would sometimes get frustrated when months would go by and we weren't discussing any development, fearing I was in denial. Then we would take another baby step.

Going out.

There was a lot of fear with that. Mostly about what people would think. Of him. Of ME being with him. If memory serves, the first time we were out in public was with one of his crossdressing friends, Victoria. We went to dinner at a TG-friendly restaurant.

It was another "non-event" to add to my accumulating library of experiences in my brain. Little by little I began to relax.

These outings grew in scale.

I now attend monthly GNO (gurls night out) events that are usually anywhere from six to twenty crossdressers and a few

Living with Crossdressing: Defining a New Normal

of us genetic women (sometimes only me, sometimes there could be two or three of us). Apparently we are the "holy grail", cis-women who accept and respect our crossdressing mates and join them out in the world.

I have attended several of their monthly parties where they take over a local bar for a closed event. Then there's the annual Gala Ball. That was a little intimidating the first time.

What have I taken away from these? I won't lie and say ALL crossdressers are squeaky-clean. Anytime you get a large group together there will be ... shall we say... "colorful" ones mixed in.

But, overall? They are people that are trying very hard to show homage to women and their forms. They dress properly and make every effort to be as passable as they can. They carry themselves with pride and dignity. All they want is to be seen as what they are presenting as...a woman.

As a result of attending these parties and dinners, I have formed friendships and bonded with many of the gurls and their partners. I MISS them when I do not attend! My world has taken a polar shift from the early days.

Does this mean I am great with all things crossdresser?

Nope. I am still a work in progress.

The layers of this particular onion are many. I am still peeling them, and will continue to do so for a long time. Some days I have frustration, other days I am ok. I still worry about Savannah being discovered unexpectedly.

I am not a fan if he tries to wear a nightie to bed or around the house. I am not a fan of his shaving body hair. We work together to find compromise and a place where we can both get what we want though. It's not fair for me to tell him how to be in his own home, what to wear...just as it's not fair for him to expect me to be OK with stubble and seeing something that makes me uncomfortable.

It's still a mystery to me why I can see Savannah in all her splendor fully made up and be ok with that...but take the man under her and just throw a nightgown on him, and its awkward and uncomfortable. I've tried to explain it to him and myself...without much luck.

It's another layer of the onion.

At this point I am comfortable that the answers will present themselves when my overloaded brain is ready to receive them. I can be patient. He has "shown, not told" so much to this point. Actions definitely speak much louder than words.

I have heard from another woman that found out about the crossdressing and went immediately into acceptance. Now, a year or two down the road, those other more difficult emotions are cropping up.

I think if I were to offer any advice it would be to just BE. Experience the emotions. Follow the path as it lies ahead.

If you want to read,... read. Read till your eyes cross.

If you need to talk,... talk. Talk yourself hoarse.

Cry, get mad, isolate...just be. Let it happen.

I find I come out the other side of these emotions with a slightly shifted perspective BECAUSE I allowed these thoughts free reign in my head. If you have fears, by all means, bring them up. Allow your crossdresser the opportunity to say their peace on the subject. As many times as you need to hear it until you believe (or not).

Paradigm shifts occur when we least expect it. It creates shifts in your perspective, your thoughts, and ideas.

The key is to have an open mind. Don't judge before the jury is out.

Love,

Jen

The Last Crusade

> *We're born alone, we live alone, we die alone. Only through our love and friendship can we create the illusion for the moment that we're not alone.*
>
> ~ Orson Welles

> *I have decided to stick with love. Hate is too great a burden to bear.*
>
> ~ Martin Luther King, Jr.

The Holy Grail

It is considered a myth; the fictional supportive and loving woman who wants to be with a crossdresser. They say these women do not exist (and who are *they*?). If there is one woman to be found, there can't be more than one in existence, right? If you are a real woman reading this book, you may be one of those people.

I am speaking now directly to the women reading this book.

You are not a myth.

You are real.

Jen is not the only woman dealing with a crossdressing man (that's me!). Within my own circle of friends in the crossdressing community, there are several couples just tryin' to work it out. In fact, I ran into three couples at the same event the other night and asked them, plus others, to share their stories with us, dear reader.

Each circumstance will be different. The way that each couple dealt with this pink elephant in the living room (or front room, if you're from the Midwest) will be different. The following testimonies will not capture the full spectrum of all of the twists and turns that you can expect as a crossdresser's partner, but they will illustrate the successes and struggles that real-life couples are going through.

First, let me apologize for all of us crossdressers.

I am really sorry we are all freaks!

Wait. What?

I am being facetious, of course, but many crossdressers believe that they are abnormal and not deserving of a true feminine identity. There are other cultures that accept crossdressing contemporaries. They go as far as to provide them their own gender class and celebrate them.

Partners, please keep in mind that it takes an almost insurmountable amount of courage to reveal our other selves to you. We risk it all in order to finally be the honest and open partner that you deserve.

All I can hope for is that these testimonies serve as exhibits to what couples can face and how obstacles can be overcome. A force of will does not determine success. It is gained through trials of fire. It is gained by opening up one's mind to appreciate another perspective. It takes understanding to realize that under it all we are just people, hanging onto and re-forging that bond of love that should transcend above all else.

Partners of crossdressing men are a unique lot of women. They tend to be strong in their own individual way. They can be outspoken, have a surety of character, and have a ferocity in life about them. I believe that is why we are drawn to you as partners. We may not be able to articulate all of the reasons why we are attracted to you, but there is a measure of spirit and strength within you that shines brightly.

And in our crossdressing community, you, dear partner, should be celebrated for just showing up. You should be adored for being the evolved beautiful creatures you are – women that that can look beyond our facades and see into our true hearts and minds.

Other Stories – A Fairytale

Relationships aren't designed for selfish individuals.
                                                    ~ unknown

A loving relationship is one in which the loved one is free to be himself to laugh with me, but never at me; to cry with me, but never because of me; to love life, to love himself, to love being loved. Such a relationship is based upon freedom and can never grow in a jealous heart.
                                                    ~ Leo F. Buscaglia

Melissa And Annabelle

Melissa is a late blooming crossdressing man with a history of trauma and a stern adolescent home life led by a domineering father. Although Melissa's father's hostility was broadly directed toward him in his teen years, he was treated very fairly as a young boy. Melissa's father valued his son's maleness while directing his scorn to Melissa's sisters. And since the sisters could not exact retribution against the father, they directed their sights on Melissa by dressing him up in their clothes.

Melissa's earliest memory of crossdressing was at age three or four. His sisters dressed him up as Annie Oakley for Halloween and took him around the neighborhood. Melissa will never know if he would have found an inherent impulse or compulsion to dress on his own, but as he grew up he did adopt an interest in crossdressing because he felt he had been indoctrinated to do so.

This led to repression and depression growing up. He was forced to deny the normalcy of how he was feeling about the act of dressing. Melissa did not fully comprehend that he had a full feminine personae until 'the ripe old age of 46'. After six years of therapy (many crossdressers need qualified therapists to help resolve the fractures in their psyche), Melissa is now thriving in his duel identities and in his involvement in the crossdressing community. With therapy and much hard work, Melissa considers himself an advanced crossdresser with the skill set to move freely about in either persona when the desire strikes. He knows who he is and what he wants out of his feminine personae, after much struggle and self-examination.

Melissa's partner, Annabelle, is a divorced mother of four. She is a creative and fluid spirit, spending most of her adult career as both a dancer and a nurse. Her exposure to the crossdressing world is by way of her many friendships and acquaintances with gay men, drag queens, and the like. She is fully invested with Melissa in both his male and female sides.

But you said that crossdressers are not typically gay or drag queens. Are you back-pedaling, now?

Good catch, dear reader. I see you are paying attention! Great job!

Misconceptions

I mentioned Annabelle's resume for a reason. Her previous experience and close contact with people with different gender identities and sexual orientations allows her to inherently understand them as people instead of just as labels. At the end of the day, the use of labels serves to bucket people into desirables and undesirables, allowing for people to rationalize a reason to dislike – or even hate – entire groups of people. It is a rationalization based on a single experience or vague understandings of what those people are about. In the end we are all just people, trying to live our lives.

Interestingly enough, in spite of her previous associations with people living alternative lifestyles, she still had plenty of misconceptions about what crossdressers are and are not. Annabelle met Melissa while he was hoping to schedule a dance class for crossdressers (and their partners).

Annabelle, before meeting all of us, thought that Melissa would be more flamboyant like the drag queens she knew. She also assumed that everyone was gay, since most of the drag queens she knew were. Those notions are difficult to shake off because those ideas have been so prevalent as labels for the typical, everyday crossdressing male.

Truth Is Not Skin Deep

Melissa and Annabelle's story is a bit different from the others we will talk about. First of all, Annabelle met Melissa as Melissa. There was no secret life to be explained or revealed. There were no shocking discoveries of Melissa's feminine side after months of courtship (yeah, I said courtship instead of dating... I'm old-fashioned). The relationship originated with truth and openness, which is already a huge positive step. Annabelle had the opportunity to decide at the outset whether or not to pursue a friendship or a partnership with Melissa.

If you talk to Melissa and Annabelle you get two conflicting perspectives. While Annabelle is drawn to Melissa's kindness, generosity, and selflessness (her words!), Melissa is agape with the wonderment of why Annabelle would grace his life in the first place. What Melissa (and many of us) fail to understand is that the partners in our lives are not there because they are attracted to our Ryan Gosling looks, but the strength and quality of our character. They see the best in us while we see our faults. It is both our physical attributes and our spirit that make up the whole of us.

For Your Consideration ~

My dad once told me a story about how he perceived beauty when he was a man in his twenties. He had an uncle with what he initially described as a very plain and homely wife. His uncle doted on and adored her. After spending a couple hours being in the presence of his aunt's kindness and positively spirited personality, my dad left with the perspective that his aunt was much prettier than he initially realized. My dad started to understand that beauty was not just the cosmetics of what we see, but the qualities that make up the whole person.

It was an interesting story. As people, we tend to be attracted to the whole person, not just the façade we first see. Beauty can get us in the door, but it is our spirit and how we treat others that dulls or illuminates that beauty.

Melissa mentioned to Jen and me that he was overly nervous for Annabelle to finally meet him as a man. He was worried that Annabelle would not be attracted to his male persona because she had only met him as Melissa. So, here we have the heel on the other foot, where the crossdresser is worried about acceptance from a possible partner because of the biology they were born into. That goes to show how we can be uncomfortable in our skin, whatever the clothing we wear.

Sometimes the clothing we wear can be freeing.
Sometimes it can serve as protective armor.
Sometimes it can be a prison sentence.

Open Book

Annabelle made the point that being with Melissa didn't change how she felt about her own sexual identity. She was initially a bit confused as she found herself attracted to Melissa since she has never had romantic inklings toward another woman or crossdresser. With a shrug of her shoulders, she says that she quickly got over that reservation and really hasn't thought of it since. She loves the person Melissa is inside, stating, "Outside doesn't really make a difference to me."

And that idea carries forward in most aspects of her life. She celebrates the things she loves. She has no fear about introducing Melissa to her family and friends. She knows she raised her girls to be open-minded, and she knows her friends are very modern- and forward-thinking individuals. Annabelle doesn't care what the rest of the people think about her and her partner. She doesn't succumb to the judgment of others, nor does she suffer those who would cast ill will toward her.

On the other beautifully manicured hand, Melissa has no interest in revealing more about himself to his own family than is absolutely necessary. In his male life, only two people are aware that he is a crossdresser. He feels that sharing the knowledge of his feminine side wouldn't enrich his life or the life of the person that would be told. For him, there needs to be a compelling reason to reveal his whole self to others. And he hasn't found that reason yet. He understands that this reasoning makes him seem aloof and cold to some people, but he seems okay with that title.

Melissa and Annabelle agreed that it was okay for Melissa to reveal himself to Annabelle's daughters. Ironically, this systematically negates his own policy of only revealing himself to a select few. Maybe the issue is that Melissa would prefer to live an open life where he'll feel the most accepted, leaving the people of his past in the past. At any rate, he feels he is living a balanced life, both with his male and female identities and with his new relationship.

Eye Of The Beholder

Today, Melissa and Annabelle bare their spirits to each other. Yes, that sounds cheesy. And you would be right. Their relationship is sickly sweet, and they are all the more adorable for it. Melissa is amazed and wonderstruck that Annabelle has total support and acceptance for him as a friend and partner. In fact, Melissa says that Annabelle accepts him more than he accepts himself, even after six years of therapy. That acceptance has been very disarming for Melissa, allowing all aspects of their relationship to flourish. So much so that Melissa has found a level of love and intimacy that he had not experienced before or thought possible.

For Melissa, Annabelle's acceptance and love for him has allowed the pieces of his life to finally fall easily into place. It is not a struggle to make their relationship work. To hear Melissa say it, "Annabelle has shown me a reflection of myself…"

Partners who live with crossdressing men can have a chaotic existence. For Melissa, therapy allowed him to gain the courage to work on his transgender issues and figure out how to accept and incorporate his feminine side into everyday life. Annabelle's acceptance of him gives Melissa validation that maybe he is (and the rest of us are) just normal folk.

Failure To Understand

I asked both of them the question of what they felt the other would never understand about them. Annabelle is surprised that she constantly has to reaffirm her love for Melissa. She can't understand why she has to explain why she loves him so much. Melissa's biggest surprise is that Annabelle has such an easy time with his female side. He can't understand why Annabelle would love him. As Melissa told us, Annabelle is "…more accepting of me than I am." Annabelle scratches her head about why Melissa is so dense about the intangibles of her feelings and emotions for him, while Melissa points out more dire points of misunderstanding between crossdressers and their partners.

Melissa believes that a cis-female partner would have difficulty understanding the rationale that a crossdressing man could be confused by their gender. He goes on to add that one of the earliest concepts a person understands beyond their existence is their biology. A boy is a boy, and a girl is a girl. But I am a boy who likes to be a girl. It's most difficult to convey how disturbing and disruptive a confusion like that can be for a youth. And trying to get anyone else to understand that frustration – especially people who did not struggle with it – is no small feat.

For Your Consideration ~

It's easier to understand the above points if you draw parallels. We crossdressers can prattle on for hours about how we were drawn to our mother's or sister's clothes and how it just made us feel safe and comforted. Our partners, however, may not be able to comprehend that specific act or line of thinking. We can ask our partners if wearing a boyfriend's jersey or varsity jacket made them feel safe and loved. Do they love to wear an old pair of sweatpants or comfy knit sweater after the workday is done?

If the answer is yes, then you can start fostering an understanding of why clothing affects our moods and emotions, either by the escapism it provides or the memories it elicits through its feel or smell.

As for Annabelle's point, I blame Melissa for his lack of understanding. Yes, I put the blame wholly on his shoulders. He's a big girl. He can take it.
That's harsh!
Not really. Melissa knows I love to tease him.
Many of us live with the perceived shame of that which we are, even after we have accepted ourselves and how our feminine sides fit into our lives. I believe that the acceptance we have for ourselves is sometimes more of a resignation or tolerance for what we are, always hoping that we would eventually go back to what society deems appropriate. And if we cannot love ourselves for who we are and the qualities we possess, how would our brains ever acknowledge that others would be so willing to accept us for

what we are.

Words Of Wisdom

In spite of Melissa's reservations about the *how's* and *whys* of Annabelle's affections for him, he does offer some pearls of wisdom from his own life experiences for how to share our feminine selves with our prospective partners. The following is simple advice but it should be understood that each relationship and participant is different.

Melissa talks about the decision to tell someone about being a crossdresser as a risk assessment exercise. *How romantic,* I would tell her with sarcasm. It is true that our crossdressing is probably the single most important facet to be divulged and shared. That being said, we have to be mindful of our partner and present the "all of us" to her in the best way. Never approach the process as if crossdressing is bad or as if you are revealing a terrible secret (even though it could be considered a terrible secret). Just try to lay out the information in a positive way.

For Your Consideration ~

> *Crossdressers, if you truly want a full and honest relationship with your partner, don't wait to tell them about yourself. Conversely, don't walk up to a beautiful women you are interested in at the bar and tell her that you crossdress as part of your pick-up line. The best course is to allow your partner to understand the kind of person you are. And you need to understand them.*

Additionally, Melissa's only regret is that he let this aspect of his life go on for so long before deciding to invest time and energy to make that side of his life better. He regrets not having the inner strength to do something about Melissa's development at a younger age.

I would tell you that nostalgia is the first step to the path of regret. Do not dwell in the past because to do so is to forget that there is a present to live in. And don't worry about the future because it is always fluid and ever changing. The most detailed planning for the future can paralyze the present.

And, In Conclusion

Melissa and Annabelle both see the best in each other. They have a spirit of character that they demonstrate every day. They are an example of instant chemistry where they shared a desire to learn all they could about each other.

Melissa is a selfless and caring partner, always wanting to take away any obstacle from Annabelle's path. He is fierce in his loyalty to her, very protective of her happiness and security. Those qualities shine through very transparently and, of course, are some of the many reasons why Annabelle is attracted to him. They both kid about fairies (not a derogatory term for an effeminate gay male) who replaced a Hoover almost overnight and who materialize a new LBDs (in one case, blue) at a moment's notice.

That's all sweet and gooey, but how do they deal with his crossdressing?

Ok... sorry, I was rambling.

For Melissa and Annabelle, there are no acceptance issues between them. They go out to both mainstream restaurants and private crossdressing events. They are a regular couple where Annabelle is just as happy to be with Melissa as with Melissa's male side. She holds no distinction between the two. In her words, "I don't care what you wear. It doesn't change who you are".

But every fairy tale is not all that interesting to the reader unless there is some sort of conflict. Their issues reside in the secrecy and status of their relationship. Annabelle's daughters have met Melissa in both male and female attire (and are fine with the fact that he is a crossdresser), but Melissa and Annabelle have kept under wraps the true nature of their relationship. They feel they need to wait until a more appropriate time for the reveal to the rest of the family. Melissa worries about how to handle a new dynamic for their finances, how a new family structure will unfold, and, you know, the usual issues that plague every red-blooded American couple.

Otherwise, they share a charmed life together.

Other Stories - Crosses to Bear

You gain strength, courage, and confidence by every experience in which you really stop to look fear in the face. You are able to say to yourself, 'I lived through this horror. I can take the next thing that comes along.'

~ Eleanor Roosevelt

If you want to conquer fear, don't sit home and think about it. Go out and get busy.

~ Dale Carnegie

Diane And Eva

Diane is a law enforcement officer. You know, one of those fields where crossdressing could be considered a bad thing? The brotherhood of police is still very much a boy's club, even in today's climate. There is plenty of hazing throughout the ranks. But as long as you go along, you get along.

He is quiet as Diane, with a shyness and reserved quality about him. He grew up in the boroughs of New York City, living with his parents and sister in a two-bedroom railroad box-style apartment. As a child he was lucky enough to sleep in the master bedroom while his younger sister got the smaller bedroom and his parents relegated themselves to sleeping in the dining room.

Diane grew up with an admiration of his mother's quiet

sacrifices to the family. He also admired his maternal grandmother's dedication and devotion to her own husband. Diane found that these women possessed a truly honorable and intangible quality that let them sacrifice for the greater good. He also envied that women could show other women tenderness with personal contact, able to drop their defenses and share honestly with each other.

When he entered into puberty, Diane was drawn to his mom's clothing and to her girdles, in particular. Was he trying to capture his mother's spirit by wearing her clothes? Did he believe that there could be transference of energy from the fabric? He didn't understand the reasons why he was drawn to his mother's things. All things sexual or sensual were still a mystery to him.

Diane grew up in the pre-Internet era, before the rites of becoming a man were spoken of openly. He is a stoic person, not looking to ask the questions, either. He felt foolish around women, always unsure of what he should be doing socially and intimately. He wasn't a bar scene player; his friends were the ones to set him up on dates. None of those girlfriends went the distance.

But something changed. While on vacation with friends, he passed up a chance to pursue a beautiful Jersey Girl because of his insecurities. He did, however, have an instant and comfortable connection to another girl living in that locale. The awkwardness he usually endured was replaced with easiness and a calm he had not experienced before.

Diane's partner Eva is a career mother and therapist. She has spent a lifetime building a family and a body of work. She is direct and honest in conversation, unafraid to speak her mind. And she can also cut loose on the dance floor all by herself when her favorite 80s jam comes out da DJ's speakers. It's a great combination.

She has worked for years intently hearing her patients' words, looking to uncover and understand what keeps them from living a fulfilled life. She has even heard tales from partners of crossdressers and had to offer them counsel on what steps to take next.

The Hanged Woman

After they married, Diane's urge to crossdress subsided for a time. But, as with many of our kind, there were cycles of purging and of buying again. Diane spent years trying to stifle his crossdressing, controlling his life, and his wife. There were some very dark times during those years. So dark, in fact, he held a fantasy where he was in the World Trade Center on September 11th when the buildings came down. That way he would have simply blinked out of existence, labeled as a hero. His secret would have been vaporized along with him and his family would have been taken care of.

Diane hated the man he was. He despised the choices he had made. He used the analogy that Eva was like a woman at the end of a hangman's noose. If you tighten the knot in the right way and place it at the correct point on the neck, the fall will instantly kill the victim. If not, the fall will only succeed in a slow strangulation. Diane felt that he was cutting off the breath of the health of his relationship with Eva, serving only to cause Eva pain and hurt.

Eva had taught Diane about the world. He had never gained that knowledge on his own growing up. In spite of expanding his understanding of the world, he continued to live in a constrictive vacuum because of his alter ego. For years, they argued as Diane tried to control every aspect of their relationship.

The figurative noose was tightening itself around Eva's neck as the perpetuation of Diane's secret added stress to their relationship. In addition, their church's teachings and society's opinion on crossdressing served to reinforce that what he was doing was wrong. In spite of all the reasons that kept him from sharing his secret, Diane found his decision to keep silent more and more deplorable. It was an internal conflict that caused him to go to many dark, empty places.

From The Frying Pan

So imagine Eva's surprise when, after thirty-two years of marriage and a very stressful personal tragic event, she found out about Diane's crossdressing. It all came to a head one evening in the bedroom when Diane uttered those often-used words, "I have something to tell you".

This type of knowledge is enlightening, but only initially and in a limited way. The crossdresser's admission illuminates the *whys* of his sometimes odd behavior. The whys of clothing being in the wrong place, tops being stretched out, remnants of makeup, strange discoveries of feminine accessories, and the like. This admission comes with the terrible new knowledge that the crossdresser has lived a lie and kept a serious secret.

And what a whopper of a secret it is. Eva didn't have any inkling that what her husband was doing was in the realm of possibility. Sure, some behavior was now explained away but other harsher paranoia crept in. If he was this adept at hiding his feminine side for all these years, then he must be a master of manipulation and a lord of lies. That is a difficult logical argument for a crossdresser to refute. Yes, it is true that most of us have become very skilled at keeping this specific secret from judging eyes and unwanted attention. Just keep in mind that this secret was and is an act of self-preservation and, maybe, shame, not of deception with the intent of malice.

From Diane's point of view, he considers Eva akin to a victim of a crime. In his experience, the victims of crime take a back seat to the investigator's focus on the crime itself. Eva lived ignorant of the identity of Diane for years. Now she was saddled with an influx of knowledge laced with more questions than answers, fears of what other secrets have been kept from her, and the realization that there was now a third person in their relationship.

Commiseration

Eva was now an accessory after the fact for the lifelong lie that Diane had orchestrated during their marriage. Now Eva knew… and was instantly forced to keep the same secret.

Who does she have to talk to?

Indeed, whom did she have to turn to? She could talk to her daughter who had discovered Diane years earlier. The two of them could commiserate about Diane, but Eva's daughter had her own burden to bear for the secret she had been forced to keep. Eva's daughter had told her sister because the secret was too big and arduous to carry alone. And she couldn't tell her mom something that should come from her dad. So who else?

A close friend of the family, Dawn, was going through her own problems with a troubled marriage and called Eva often to vent her anger and hope for sympathy. She would tell Eva that she was so envious of what Eva and her husband had in their more-perfect marriage. While Dawn was lamenting all of the details of her difficult relationship, Eva could only offer generalities about the problems she also was going through.

Eva asked Diane to tell Dawn the truth so that Eva would not have to stilt their conversations. Diane agreed, but the opportunity for the reveal came and went without execution. Eva's tenuous trust in Diane took a hit as a result; she was feeling betrayed that he didn't physically follow through with his promise.

On a positive note, once Eva and Diane started venturing out together she did meet other married couples facing the same situation in their own relationship. They attended group meetings where they could share their story and hear the trials and tribulations that other couples were facing. It helped Eva to realize that her problems were not unique and that she could lean on others for advice and empathy.

For Your Consideration ~

> *It is important to note that words are just words. If those words are not supported by actions, they become meaningless. And if more promises are given without action, those words become bigger daggers of mistrust and doubt.*

Stand By Your Man

Jen and I met them for the first time at our second Femme Fever Gala Ball weekend, sitting next to Dane and Eva at Applebee's during lunch. At the time, we thought they were a stable crossdressing couple. What we didn't know is that Eva had just found out about Diane mere months before. But here she sat at a long table lined with crossdressers (and some partners), out in the daylight for the world to see... or at least other patrons that would never know them in real life.

One of the things we crossdressers sometimes forget is that our partner is always going to be who she is. While we crossdressers can hide under our makeup and counter-intuitive feminine clothing, our partners are faced with the issue of simply being themselves. What if you go out to a local restaurant as a couple and happen to run into old friends who recognize your partner straight away? It doesn't take long for them to connect the dots.

IF
Partner A is out with Girlfriend B
AND
Girlfriend B looks similar to Husband C of Partner A
THEN Girlfriend B is Husband C.

I think it may be Einstein's theory of femininity.

Jen, who was also new to the idea of facing the sunlight with a crossdressing partner, felt inadequate as she and Eva spoke. Eva appeared so at ease with Diane as they perused the menus and talked about what to order, while Jen was struggling with her acceptance of me and us as a public couple.

Eva may have seemed at ease, but she was dealing with her anger and fear. For one, she was not the first to know about Diane. As I had mentioned earlier, her daughter already knew, catching Diane dressing at their home four years earlier. Having only seen a glimpse of Diane, this young woman thought that her dad was having an affair with this new woman. Diane was forced to admit that he was *that woman*.

On a side note, Diane mentioned to us that he was happy to have come away unscathed from his daughter's discovery of his femininity. Diane left his daughter to her own thoughts and struggles to understand what she had witnessed. Selfishly, Diane did not pursue other conversations with his daughter; did not try to delve deeper into helping his daughter with her peace of mind. It is one of Diane's regrets where he had talked himself into believing that everything was fine.

Finally, four years later after a tragic and unexpected death in the family, Diane found he was sick of the lies he had told and the secrets he was keeping. He was devastated and couldn't keep who he was to himself anymore. With sincerity and conviction, Diane told Eva about his crossdressing. Eva listened to her husband with her whole heart, knowing that the words her husband spoke were the truth. The words were sincere and filled with pained emotion. In spite of her fears and reservations, she looked at her husband with fresh eyes – maybe clinical eyes – and decided to support her husband's activities.

To Eva he was a good husband, a good provider, and a good father. She thought that she owed it to Diane to be a good wife. Was it her years as a therapist and the stories she had listened to from the patients on her couch that gave her a softened and supportive perspective? Was it a fear of losing what she had built over the years? Was it an interesting and novel experiment?

Adult Novelties

In fact, it was a novel and interesting experiment between them for a time. The relief of finally sharing a terrible burden allowed Diane to be more present and calm. Eva, without understanding the magnitude of what her husband's crossdressing meant, got a kick and kinky pleasure out of their romantic exploits. They went shopping together for clothes and wigs where Eva got to pretend that the articles for purchase were for her, not her husband. It was a risqué and adventurous time.

But that interest and excitement faded – as with many new toys. One day, Eva was kissed by Diane and became confused and conflicted. She didn't like the fact that she was kissing another woman – faux or otherwise. Eva didn't consider, or want to consider, herself a lesbian. Her crossdressing husband didn't turn her on when he was wearing lingerie or a dress. She wanted her man to be a man, have hair on his body, and be her husband.

Diane wanted to be smooth, so the negotiations started. Where do you draw the line? The lines are different for different couples. You have to be conscious of supporting the other's needs as well as your own. In the case of Diane and Eva, he was able to shave all over, with the exception of a certain manly attributed area south of the border.

On a vacation to a warm climate, Eva worried that everyone would be staring at Diane's shaved legs. She feared the judgment and questions that she would have to explain away with more lies. In the end, those fears were baseless as no one noticed or even cared enough to ask about his lack of hair.

The Greatest Fear

But other fears are always lurking in the back corners of the mind; always simmering under the surface of an otherwise calm pond. During our interview, Diane was very direct and honest when offering a perspective that he hoped would help other struggling couples. During that first year of exploration and public appearances, they went to a week-long event in Provincetown called Fantasia Fair. The floodgates for their emotions were opened wide.

During that seven-day event, the crossdressers had the freedom to dress all week, day and night. To Eva, the event was a sacrifice that she had made for her husband so that he could be comfortable and happy. It was all going to be about Diane that week. And it was all about Diane… for a while.

During segregated breakout meet and greets, the crossdressers and other alternative gender identified individuals grouped together. Diane was experiencing a sense of euphoria, finally in a safe and accepting environment. There were so many other crossdressers to interact with; so much time to enjoy the freedom of presenting as a woman.

Eva and the other partners met, too. They shared their stories, fears, and heart-wrenching struggles. The cork of their pent-up emotions popped and the tears of pain, frustration and gratitude were wholly unleashed.

Once the couples were brought back together in a later session, Diane, after seeing his wife and the other partners, realized that his enjoyment of his feminine freedom came with a huge emotional cost that Eva was continuing to pay. Diane, in his telling of his secret to Eva and their subsequent exploration, didn't realize (or want to acknowledge) that the secret shared wasn't shared equally. Diane had unburdened the shame of all of his secrecy; by adding it to Eva's already taxed shoulders.

At the end of the week, everyone came together for the last session of the event. In this forum, they were afforded the opportunity to say how they felt or what they had learned. Diane stood up and acknowledged that he would be happy to get back to his male life for a while, feeling overwhelmed by the excessive amount of time spent as *her* that week. During the exit from the conference room, a transsexual woman approached him. She grabbed his arm and declared "…this was not the end for Diane", that Diane would "…want much more".

This woman's words scared him. What did it mean to him? Was Diane being obtuse in his belief that crossdressing was all that he wanted, that he would never want to transition to a female later on? Diane admitted that he had become adept at only seeing what he wanted to see and ignoring everything else. He likens the feeling to the Simon and Garfunkel song, *The Boxer*, where they sing "…a man hears what he wants to hear, and disregards the rest."

Hearing these words from her husband's mouth was the realization of one of Eva's fears. Now, she was finding this out for the first time in front of Jen and me. Eva pointed out that they should have had this conversation in private. Eva told him she expected honesty and disclosure from her husband. She told him she needed to be a part of the discussion, not just a recipient of decisions made. Hearing that the transsexual woman's words had so impacted Diane caused Eva to well up with anger and fear. Her resentment at being lied to for years was validated with what she considered more deception.

Outside Perspective

The tension between Eva and Diane was palpable. I reiterated what I interpreted that they each said. Jen answered Eva's question, "What do you think of this? Is it fair?" with "It is unfair to hear it this way, but remember that in the end you have control to make the decision to stay or go." We wanted to make sure that they realized that we were honored that Diane felt safe and comfortable enough to speak up about his fears on the subject, and respectful of Eva's feelings of fear on the subject matter.

For Your Consideration ~

Please understand that trying to discover who we are as crossdressers is an impossible task if you can't take a serious hard look inside yourself.

After that evening, Eva and Diane spent several weeks discussing the issue of male-to-female transitioning. For Eva, it is an absolute that she be given an equal voice in the relationship. She is Diane's wife, an equal partner in all matters. She has the right to decide what she is willing to commit to. It is her choice whether to stay for *the death do us part* part, or to decide to leave in pursuit of her own fulfilled life. She didn't sign up for having a part-time girlfriend... so thinking about a full-time version raises all of its own issues and consequences.

Eva doesn't want to look back on a life half-lived. She worries that a time may come when she discovers that she has been duped into believing in her husband's *lies*. Ignorance may not be lying. Lying to yourself, however, can hurt those around you.

Communion

Another interesting note is Eva's perspective of intimacy with Diane. After that initial run of risqué adventure with Diane and the subsequent intimate back-pedaling due to Eva's discomfort of being with another *woman*, Eva continued to offer intimate moments to her husband's alter ego.

Why?

Although not turned on by the feminine presentation of Diane, Eva feels that it is important to show Diane affection and physical interaction. She does it out of love for her husband and for the life they have built together. There also might be a little fear that if she doesn't, Diane could seek that intimacy outside the marriage. By doing so, Eva is exhibiting that feminine selflessness that Diane so admires.

For Your Consideration ~

> *I was skeptical about Eva's reasoning because I am always concerned if my partner is doing something out of obligation. I believe forced obligation leads to resentments. Jen told me to look at it a different way. She says that doing something out of a sense of obligation can be performed because of their love for their partner. In a relationship, we all sacrifice something to make our partner happy. We freely give of ourselves to demonstrate our affection.*

Antiquated Notions

Eva doesn't want to hold back Diane, but she doesn't want Diane to hold her back, either. The years of just accepting whatever the situation was in their marriage is over. Diane, in his attempts to control his own life, controlled Eva's life by keeping her ignorant of the household finances, investments, and decision-making. Diane's crossdressing secret caused a stranglehold on the relationship, keeping every facet of it as precise as possible. The pressure of controlling the relationship helped to fracture it. With Diane's admission and a newfound (or rediscovered) sense of self, Diane and Eva continue to talk it out, hug it out, and do whatever else they need to do to make their new dynamic work.

Mistaken Identities

We have met up with Diane and Eva at GNO dinners at TG-friendly restaurants. They attend private long island events and the annual Femme Fever Gala Ball. Eva is the more outspoken one when talking about their relationship, quick and happy to share their trials and tribulations. Some of their issues are universal to all relationships involving crossdressers and their partners.

One of Eva's complaints is of being mistaken for a crossdressing man. She is woman… hear her roar! What self-respecting cis-woman wants to be looked over and be thought to be a crossdressing or transitioning man? In a sea of crossdressers, the real women may feel they fall short in their own feminine presentation. How in the heck do you compete with men who put hours into their expression? How do you compare transsexuals who have better breasts than you do?

Eva was shocked at her resentment toward Diane for taking ninety minutes or more to get ready to go out. Eva had been previously happy to whip herself together in ten to twenty minutes. Now, she started to wonder about the efforts she was putting in for herself. Eva said she "...was shamed into taking better care of herself".

For Your Consideration ~

Comfort may breed complacency. Why try to put in the extra effort when you have already secured your man?

Crossdressing men are in constant pursuit of the ultimate feminine expression. We woman-watch to see what they are wearing, how they wear it, and how we could incorporate those elements into our own presentation.

Women, be the best you can be. Do not do it for others but for yourself. Crossdressers only wish that they could be feminine like you in the easy way that you can. Regardless of your weight, age, or shape, you are always going to have the natural attributes to be something that we cannot achieve without hard work.

The Future Is Now

What does Eva want from their relationship as they move forward into an uncertain future? She is looking for honesty and respect. She hopes that she and Diane can be happier in all aspects

Living with Crossdressing: Defining a New Normal

of their relationship. She wants them to be able to have fun and lead a more carefree existence. She wants less arguments, secrets, and tension. In a nutshell, Eva wants her husband Diane to be her best friend. For Diane, he strives to understand how to be a better husband, *woman* and partner. He still wants to become that devoted and selfless partner that he saw his mother and grandmother be all those years earlier.

Diane and Eva want what all couples want in their relationship when they look back on the phases of their lives together. They want to have what they had at the beginning. They want to recapture that passion and love that instantly connected them all those many years ago under a summer sun on tropical beach sand.

What had they lost?

They want spontaneity, passion and love for life and for each other. They want a selfless idealism about the world that has suffered and eroded over the years. The decay of those positive parts of themselves led to them to forget the reasons why they loved life – and why they loved each other.

Diane's crossdressing secret was at the nexus of troubles that contributed to their relationship's state of emergency. His obsessive-compulsive disorder played its part to add tension to their union. The passing of time, the passing away of parents, the rigors and joys of having children, the typical complacencies that descend on any relationship of great length, taking each other for granted... all fester and grow in the corners of any marriage spanning decades. It is not unique to only couples dealing with crossdressing.

Over the years, Diane's secret made his life more interesting and exciting. Because he found that he didn't really like the man who stared at him in the mirror each morning anymore, he hid that face behind foundation and a wig to escape his existence for a few hours at a time. But during the return to manhood, Diane felt guilty and dirty about his pleasure. He felt he was cheating on Eva.

Diane wants to erase the hurt he has caused his wife, and not be an instrument of additional pain as they move forward. He wants them to remember that spontaneity they once shared before this secret, his OCD, and disillusionment started to crush their spirits. He wants to understand women; to understand how they can be so selfless and sacrificing. Diane believes there is something of purpose in their future. Just as they used to volunteer and help others, he feels that there is something from their current truth that can assist others facing the same dilemmas.

Can these dreams be something that can be actualized beyond the simple act of hoping? I believe there is always hope... and that hope can be realized. It just takes commitment, perseverance and understanding. In Eva's own words, "If there is true understanding and awareness, change can be made."

Other Stories – Late To The Party

Whoever is careless with the truth in small matters cannot be trusted with important matters.

~ Albert Einstein

Everything we hear is an opinion, not a fact. Everything we see is a perspective, not the truth.

~ Marcus Aurelius

Debra And Eden

Debra is a jeweler in his 60s who discovered at the age of ten that there was such a thing as crossdressing men. He saw a photograph of a beautiful woman in a newspaper (you know, that thick paper that is filled with articles, sports stats, and comic strips?). Then he read the caption under the photo that said that the woman was a female impersonator. Debra was captivated that a man could look so desirable and alluring.

Prior to that moment, Debra was unaware that a boy could or should dress as a girl. In the coming weeks and months, he started to find himself drawn to the tights and underwear of his older sister. Unlike me, he never dared to break the sanctity of his mother's dresser drawers.

He never looked back. Pantyhose and panties were his clothing of choice. They provided him with both comfort and sexual release. Debra continued in this way for most of his life, only the sexual component waning in recent years.

In marriage he hid his femme accessories in the bottom of his closet and in the garage, where prying eyes would never find them. Any time he had a few hours in an empty house, he would put on his panties, slide the pantyhose up his legs, and be in bliss.

Debra wife, Eden, is a woman also in her 60s, although she looks a bit younger than her years denote. She and her sister were a bit nomadic in their youth, bouncing around from house to house due to an ever-changing family dynamic. Eden is a mother of two beautiful married girls, one of them with a child. But those are just statistics.

Like Eden from the Old Testament, Eden thirsts for knowledge. She is a reader with a love of gothic horror. Eden wrote her thesis on Edgar Allan Poe. She finds H.P. Lovecraft's work grotesque and fascinating. Bags full of books are stored in her basement from years of enjoyment.

Eden was a career woman in her early adult life. She thought for a moment to pursue a career in law, but decided on going into the publishing field instead. She worked for a major magazine for seven years before finally giving it up to bring up their two daughters.

When the girls were older, Eden did not return to the world of publishing but did find satisfaction with a decade of work in children's retail and then ten years as a medical secretary. She always found something to keep her mind and body busy, even volunteering at her synagogue for many years. By October of 2015, Eden had decided that maybe retirement was her next adventure.

Boiling Point

In a snowy January of 2016, Eden's daughter was deep into her pregnancy. There was a threat of a massive snowstorm. Eden, perhaps with a woman's and a mother's intuition, felt a need to go into the city to be with her daughter. It was lucky she did because her daughter soon went into labor.

Eden called Debra, who worked in the city, to see if he wanted to come over. Worried that his car may be stuck in drifts of snow if left in the Long Island Railroad parking lot, Debra decided to fetch it and stay home alone that night.

Debra spent that night dressed. But he was not just wearing the panties and pantyhose that had been his mainstay for over 50 years. Five years prior, Debra found that it wasn't enough to just dress in those things. He started ordering more clothes and having them delivered to work. He would bring them home, hide them until Eden was out of the house, and try on whatever outfits he had purchased. Debra hadn't advanced to applying makeup, but was dressing more completely. Maybe due to psychological or hormonal changes, his sexual need to dress had diminished as he explored this new level of femininity.

Debra did go to the hospital on Sunday to be with the family and see his first grandchild. Eventually, he and Eden found themselves home again with the new identities as grandparents. That changes a person. There is an appreciation of life being drawn into the world. There is a sense that things are changing. Time is passing. The frailty of life is more evident.

Even before the birth of his grandchild, Debra had become increasingly distant in his relationship with his wife. With Eden's retirement and his dressing escalation, he felt trapped and unfulfilled with his advancing femininity. Debra's opportunities to dress had decreased and his frustration had increased. He wanted to tell Eden about the dressing, but kept losing the courage to speak the words.

Critical mass was imminent.

Finally, in April, Debra was able to utter those dreaded words, "I have something to tell you that is going to rock your world." Eden braced for the worst news she could imagine – cancer, foreclosure, lost savings, an affair, or the want of a divorce. But none of those things were true.

Debra revealed that what he had been doing for all of those years was wearing panties and pantyhose. He admitted that he was now dressing more completely. Eden's reaction was one of relief. None of the terrible possibilities she had dreamed up in her panic were true. The revelation of her husband being a crossdresser seemed like a blessing in comparison.

But Eden needed to brace herself again as the floodgates of new information opened. Debra revealed his hiding spots in the closet and the garage. He showed Eden the things he was wearing when she was out of the house and gave her a history of his dressing over the years.

Shifting Dynamics

So, how did Eden handle the reveal?

Eden and Debra both admitted that their married life had lost its luster over the last several years. Of course, this can happen to any relationship or marriage after decades together. We lose focus on our spouse. We forget to have gratitude and a love for the beautiful creature before us. We become comfortable and complacent.

In the case of many (probably most) crossdressers who keep a secret for so long from their partners, the sharing of the secret is like an anchor lifted off their hearts and minds. As the partner expresses their love and support for the tortured crossdressing man in their life, a rush of air finally escapes and the pressure that had been building finally hisses out to dissipate in the room. Debra felt lighter now that the secret was shared.

Eden, after so many years with Debra, was relieved that crossdressing was the worst the reveal included. She embraced her husband and told him that it would be all right. Eden was a woman with close gay relatives. She had sympathy for this new Caitlyn Jenner who wasn't able to live as her authentic self until so late in life. Eden understood all this and wanted her husband to feel accepted.

But Eden's reality was still rocked, as we can all imagine it would be after forty years of marriage. Eden set up the ground rule that she did not want to *see* Debra, relegating to the bedroom when her husband was dressed. Slowly, that restriction softened to having Debra give Eden notice when he wanted to dress so that she could be prepared. Eventually, that was abolished to allowing Debra to dress in the house whenever he wanted. Eden said it like this in the interview; "She should be able to dress when she wants. It's her house, too."

And while all of these ground rules were being refined, Eden went back to doing what she loved to do… read and learn. She started using the Internet to educate herself on the subject of crossdressing men. She downloaded book after book on the subject, trying to pinpoint where Debra fell on the spectrum of the transgender community.

Unfortunately, as with most things, crossdressing is not an easy thing to categorize. Debra had a lifelong pantyhose fetish that only had recently morphed into a full feminine identity. He had slid through more than one crossdressing category. Even during the interview, he acknowledged that his femme name was only a necessity because he needed a first name in order to fill in an online profile for a crossdressing site.

Debra and Eden debated and argued the merits of who should be told about *her*. Do the daughters need to know? Is it going to be a problem if the daughters decide to tell their husbands? What about Debra's older sister of whom he had borrowed her tights and panties years ago? Eden needed a have a support system for herself and her wellbeing (since there still is a scarcity of active support online or locally for the significant others of crossdressers). Reading will only take you so far, and that reading will present you with two more questions for every one it answers.

Shameless plug: Please visit LivingWithCrossdressing.com for more resources and support.

When Jen and I met Eden, we were surprised that she was so elated to meet us. Not because we are extraordinary people (although we are!), but because Eden thirsted for interaction with others who understood what she was going through. In fact, Eden started firing off questions to us as soon as we sat down to the wonderful lunch she prepared for us. We gave Eden and Debra all the information we had based on our own relationship struggles and successes. It was a good afternoon for sharing and fellowship.

Truth Be Told

As with any secret that is finally revealed, there is both an upside and a downside. The crossdresser is finally baring his soul to his partner about this secret shame, having that weight lifted off his chest. The partner finally starts to understand his true nature. The downside comes in the feelings of betrayal. She thought she knew him. After the dust settled and the shock dissipated, she was now going through her own stages of grief.

Debra was surprised in many ways by Eden's reaction to his revelation. He was floored by her acceptance of his crossdressing, but he was also surprised by her subsequent feelings of anger. Now that he had finally revealed himself to her – and that she *accepted* him – Debra thought that everything was okay. He did not understand why Eden could have such anger in her heart as a result of his admission. He failed to understand that, in spite of their history and love, this was something new to be processed.

Eden was, of course, supportive of the husband she loved. If crossdressing was the worst admission that Debra had to share, it was something that Eden felt she could rally back from. She sympathized with a person struggling with his own identity and with the burden of not being his true self. In fact, she started to push Debra to crossdress when there was an opportunity at night, frustrated that Debra was not taking advantage of the new time available to dress.

For Your Consideration ~

> *It is common for crossdressing men to just be not in the mood to dress from time to time. It does take a lot of preparation for*

some of us to transform and sometimes we are just too lazy or tired to put the effort in. It's like taking a 12-hour road trip to visit family for an afternoon. You really want to see your folks, but the effort to do so just doesn't make it seem worthwhile.

The realization that her husband kept this knowledge from Eden for so many years was sobering. Why had he felt the need to keep his crossdressing secret from her? As with other couples, where the revelation comes after so much time has passed, the women can feel that they never truly knew their partner at all. As Debra showed Eden all of his hiding spots for his feminine clothes, Eden's thoughts start racing about what else he had kept from her.

Was he really sick that day when the family was getting together or was it an excuse to stay home to dress?

Is the dressing more important to him than she is?

Is he being honest about other facets of his life?

Eden worried that Debra continued to hold something back, believing that Debra had other secrets to be revealed when he felt pressed to share them. There may be good or bad reasons to withhold information, but Eden felt she deserved to know all there was to know.

One time Eden found a text message on Debra's phone. It was an ongoing correspondence with another crossdresser where risqué digital pictures had been exchanged. What did this mean in relation to Debra's crossdressing? Was there an attraction to other crossdressers beyond simple envy and admiration? Was Debra bordering on something more sexual with another crossdressing man?

As a result of this new private message discovery, Eden's affection toward Debra had diminished. They lived under the same roof, comfortable enough with each other after four decades of marriage. As our interview hit the third hour we did note them curled up together on the other end of the sectional couch.

Eden was already struggling with one admission by her husband. Now she had to deal with this second discovery of a more sexual nature. It supported her initial fear of what crossdressing was all about. Eden felt she would be forced to discover more, learn more. Is this just the tip of the iceberg of the secrets that Debra had inside? Were there more truths to be told? She didn't think so until she read those text messages.

So, there was more processing and conversation to be had.

There was more trust to rebuild.

For Debra, he held another shared secret. That is the one of unresolved shame. He considered what he had done through the years reprehensible. The act of sexual release by wearing women's underwear, to him, was wrong. It was a compulsion that he could never shake. The shame drove the secrets deeper. If one cannot embrace their own thoughts and make peace with them, how could someone else see those thoughts as anything but utterly despicable?

Debra has a ways to go in self-acceptance, especially since he has emerged more fully as Debra in both name and physical identity. He needs to understand what he wants out of the experiences and where he wants his journey to lead. And Debra needs to share those thoughts with Eden in an honest way if there is to be hope for a stronger partnership between them.

Eden wants to be able to make her own choices with the best information available. To believe that this situation is happening to her – not with her – makes Eden question just how important she is to Debra in the vast scheme of their relationship.

Coping Mechanisms

Debra and Eden cope day to day in their relationship and their own individual mental health. Eden has her daughters to confide in. And her daughters are supportive of both of their parents, wanting their parents to be happy and their father to be safe when he is out in public.

By May, Debra had his first full makeover at FemmeFever on Long Island and finally discovered what a fully realized Debra could look like. While Debra will always have a desire and love for his pantyhose – they serve as both something sensual and as compression support while on his feet all day at work – he prefers to dress as a more complete woman when the opportunity arises.

Eden went with Debra to the Fantasia Fair in Provincetown where they spent every day with Debra dressed en femme. They met other couples that were experiencing the same issues in their own marriages. Eden wants to go out with Debra to local events but fears they may cross paths with neighbors or friends. She also doesn't attend the monthly private events, wanting Debra to have some freedoms without him feeling like he is being held back.

Eden wishes that there were more resources out there to help her cope. In spite of her love for her husband, the shock and anger inherent with discovering this truth after being together so long under such pretense requires outside support. There are CDSO (crossdresser significant others) groups out there in some metropolitan areas and online, but they are not as active and current as they could be. Plus, every situation is unique for the crossdresser and for the dynamic of the relationship with their partners. If and when you get a response from one of these groups, the answer may not be received as quickly as your reeling mind and aching heart requires or you may not get a satisfactory answer to your question at all. Eden would love to have found a CDSO group that could have been moderated by both an active crossdresser and a significant other of a crossdresser.

After a year, Eden is still coping with who her husband is. It is not a 24/7 effort anymore. She has her good days of acceptance and bad days where her acceptance wanes a bit. The issue of trust is always a big part of the equation. In those times, Eden lets those emotions come through and have their moment. It is dangerous to let those feelings bottled up without release.

I asked Eden if she felt that she was *just* surviving. Her response was that some days she feels she is just going through the motions of coexistence with Debra. Other days, she feels hope that their relationship can weather the storm and come out the other side stronger.

In the end, Eden is simply reacting to what she has been told. For her, she feels that it's up to Debra to get in touch with his repressed feelings, and for him to freely share openly and honestly. Whether that is something that can be done between them or with counseling has yet to be seen.

Eden only wants Debra to acknowledge that she is his life partner. Like with Diane and Eva in our previous story, Eden wants to come first. Not all the time, mind you, just some of the time. There needs to be a balance where each of them gets to be in the spotlight.

Crossdressing can be a very selfish act. For many of us, the focus is on one's self when transforming and perfecting the feminine presentation. But that should not blind us to the needs of our partner. Their world has been turned upside down by learning we are crossdressers. But they stayed anyway. Eden told us that she thinks about Debra when she is shopping, trying to think of something nice to buy either for her husband or for the new girlfriend in her life. The least any of us crossdressers can do is shower our partners with gratitude, affection, and gifts of the love and appreciation we have for them.

You Can Quote Me On That

Eden is very articulate and learned. She is empathetic and sincere. And she is very quotable. I had to stop our interview a couple of times so that I could get her words written down just right.

When illustrating how I see a life in balance, Eden and I collaborated that the multiple pans of the scale must have equal value, not equal weight. One pan can be weighed down heavily against the others but as long as the other pans are lighter in weight but heavier in value, the balance is still okay. Remember that a $100 bill is much lighter than a roll of quarters.

When asked if Debra was balanced, he agreed that he was. He had shed and shared the burden of his secret shame, found support and a measure of understanding, and found a newfound sense of self.

For Eden, she is operating in a "work in progress" mode. She has some good days of acceptance, some ambivalent days of tolerance, and some bad days undercut by a sense of betrayal. Eden seemed surprised when Jen concurred with her that she also goes through days that skirt between acceptance and tolerance. Just because our partners love us, that doesn't necessarily mean that they have the constant fortitude to deal with something that is still a bit foreign to them. Crossdressers, remember to have as much patience and support for your partners as they have for you.

Eden put supporting her husband's identity as Debra in the following words, "Why would someone want to live a more difficult life when they don't need to." Sure, why would Debra want to live a life where there is so much prejudice and misunderstanding against him? Society still doesn't accept the notion that crossdressers are *born that way* like they believe for gay and lesbian people and transitioning individuals. In her love for her husband, Eden realizes that Debra needs to live a full life, as he understands it.

On the flip side, Eden also said, "Better to stay with the devil you know." Debra is still battling his own demons for accepting Debra as part of his life. He continues to wrestle with an ingrained sense of shame for who he desires to be. Whether having a pantyhose fetish or going out of the house completely en femme, Debra is still shy of finding his true balance.

Eden has built a life with her husband, mothering two beautiful daughters, enjoying the new life in her grandchild, and having a home and partnership. She is not looking to jump ship at the notion of this new dynamic with Debra. What she does want is for Debra to be more attentive, more present in their relationship, and to show her a measure of gratitude and caring on the same level as Debra does for her own identity.

Eden and Debra want to have a complete and happy life together. They have built much over the years. They want the new truth to enrich and strengthen their love, not continue to repress the unknown opportunities that could be in store for them. The labor toward happiness shouldn't feel like work, but you do have to put effort in.

Living with Crossdressing: Defining a New Normal

Other Stories – Amanda…

Without a struggle, there can be no progress.
   ~ Frederick Douglas

All life demands struggle. Those who have everything given to them become lazy, selfish, and insensitive to the real values of life. The very striving and hard work that we so constantly try to avoid is the major building block in the person we are today.
   ~ Pope Paul VI

Disclaimer

This is the story of another crossdresser and his wife. In this case, though, the story is told strictly through the eyes of a man named Amanda. His wife is unaware of Amanda. Their two small boys are unaware of Amanda. Only Amanda is aware of Amanda. I wanted to include his story to hopefully illustrate what many gurls go through while holding tight to their secret femininity. While the other couples we have met continue to fight the good fight after the husbands revealed their crossdressing to their wives, Amanda's story serves as a reminder for what it is like to still be struggling with the secret.

I can relate to him a lot in terms of th intensity of the desire the balance of man/crossdresser & fear but not the internet stuff.

Living with Crossdressing: Defining a New Normal

What's The Joke?

For Amanda, the first urge to dress came around the age of four. He was fascinated by his cousin's Sunday church-going Mary Janes. He really wanted to try on her shoes, but somehow knew better than to say anything. His second encounter came at Halloween (you know, the crossdressers' Christmas) at the age of five. His mom had dressed him as his favorite childhood character, He-Man. Because of the worry of cold weather, Amanda's mom bought him a pair of tights to wear with the costume. He tried them on as soon as he got home. The weather did not turn cold so Amanda did not get to wear the tights and, eventually, the tights disappeared from his dresser drawer.

Then came third grade and the first of two pranksters at school. One of Amanda's friends dressed up as a girl as a joke. When he saw his friend, Amanda felt funny and tingly and wished that he had been the one to dress up. In the fifth grade, another friend had dressed on a lark. Amanda had lain in bed for months thinking about dressing up in something girly, and curiosity finally got the best of him. He started to try on his mom's and his younger sister's stuff.

This routine went on for a couple of years, whenever he was home alone. As elementary school became middle school, so came the changes that a young boy experiences as he becomes a teenager. Dressing became more frequent as he discovered new feelings that came with the act. Being alone was always a good excuse to wear something pretty.

Amanda thought that by high school's end he had this whole crossdressing fetish beat. But his secret life came at a price as I keep saying (I need a different line!). He really didn't date much throughout high school. He had one girlfriend, but that only lasted for a couple of months. Amanda partially feared she would find out about his crossdressing. The rest was a lack of self-confidence based on the fact that he felt so alien and different. So even well into his twenties, Amanda was not socially comfortable with other women, having more success and acceptance inside the tendrils of the digital web.

The advent of the Internet, AOL, and his own computer led to new discoveries. The cat of curiosity got the best of him once again, leading to the transgender and crossdressing sites of Geocities. Amanda would lie about his age and make up fantasies abut what he was wearing. He enjoyed the flattery and loved the validation in the chatrooms. He had constructed a virtual avatar before it was a thing, feeling at home and accepted.

Looking back on those wonder years, Amanda considered himself a fairly typical kid. He loved sports, both as a spectator and a participant. He generally liked all the things that boys are supposed to like. In college, he drank and partied (and studied) when he wasn't online. He believes that he was reasonably popular among his peers, but admits that all that time surfing the Internet probably didn't help to develop his confidence, social skills and social life. Those were good years, all in all.

Love At First Flight

Amanda first met Catherine in grade school where they shared classes together. At that age, playing and talking together was always full of innocence. Amanda says he was playfully flirting with her. Catherine admitted to Amanda that she had a crush on him, even back then. As with most things throughout adolescence,

Living with Crossdressing: Defining a New Normal

Amanda and Catherine only interacted in class or at events that kept them in close proximity. They said hello passing each other in the school hallways.

Fast-forward several years to when the high school reunion was looming. Catherine was on the reunion committee and found Amanda through social media since he had moved away from his hometown for a few years. According to Amanda, Catherine was persistent in keeping their conversations going through Facebook.

Months later, when Amanda came home to visit his family for the holidays, he and Catherine met for drinks with some friends. A few months later, Amanda and Catherine met again a few times and ended up shutting down each restaurant chatting and enjoying each other's company. Next, they spent a romantic weekend at Amanda's apartment. Once they officially started dating, much money was spent on airfare to get together once or twice a month.

It is important to remember why a husband loves his wife so much. I asked Amanda to write down the reasons why. The first reason Amanda cited was that Catherine knew what she wanted out of life and went after it. Amanda admired that in her, having struggled with confidence at times.

Catherine also represented an intellect and a different way of looking at things that Amanda found attractive. They connected on a more cerebral level. He did not get that from the people he surrounded himself with as he grew up. Catherine was worldlier and brought that worldview to him.

Aside from intelligence, Catherine possessed assertiveness and dominance concerning romantic desires and needs. Catherine initiated many of their romantic interludes. Amanda found it a turn-on, admitting that he wasn't the take-charge type when it came to matters between the sheets. His appreciation of her aggressive nature also stemmed from his fear of being rejected, relieving him from having to voice anything about his own needs and desires.

Catherine epitomized the qualities that Amanda wished he possessed. She was fearless, adventurous, and had no qualms about asking for what she wanted. Amanda first realized he was physically and emotionally attracted to her on their first NYC weekend together. They were down at the Battery in Lower Manhattan on an abnormally cold day, Catherine shivering from being underdressed for the weather. Amanda held her close the whole night to keep her warm.

Then came that first kiss.

First comes love.

Then comes marriage.

Then, yes, you guessed it, comes baby in a baby carriage.

Amanda Becomes Real

For a long time in his teenage years and early twenties, *Amanda* manifested as purely a sexual thing. Even then, there was a lot of denial and shame about what he was doing. These negative feelings retarded any true development of Amanda as a fully realized identity.

He had been on the Internet for years, with the concept of Amanda slowly gaining steam. *She* continued to lurk in the background, prowling about and not really corresponding with anyone in the real world. It has only really been in the last five years that he accepted the label of crossdresser and allowed Amanda to be expressed in a more meaningful way. But with marital restrictions and responsibilities, Amanda is, for the most part, still mainly expressed via the Internet.

Amanda has accepted his feminine half as part of who he is. He understands that he needs to have an outlet to express *her*. He longs for more quality time for Amanda, although not necessarily anything more permanent. He largely enjoys life as a male, as a husband, and as a provider.

Amanda's one hope is to express his feminine side more often; be more visible. *She* allows him to cast away the everyday stresses and live in the moment, to take a deep breath, and to let loose the femininity that helps to keep him in balance.

Balancing Acts

Is Amanda balanced?

At the moment, Amanda would say the answer is no.

Not being able to dress adds a layer of frustration to a life that is wrought with a stressful career and a wife and two boys that deserve his attention. Allowing Amanda time out for an hour or two allows him to get *her* out of his system for a while.

It's like an addict's fix, in a way. Suppressing those needs to be feminine is like holding back the waves of a tsunami with a $2 umbrella. Setting time aside for dressing allows him to think more clearly and be a better man. He needs to keep in touch with his feminine side in order to have a better perspective on life and to quell the screaming feminine demands inside his head.

Amanda is quick to point out that his crossdressing is not the only aspect of his life that keeps him off balance. First and foremost, there are his two boys. The children scream for their own attention, both literally and figuratively. They drastically alter the spousal relationship, severely constraining the time and energy for romance and intimacy with his wife.

From two childbirths, to losing an unborn child, to two periods of job upheavals and career uncertainty, relocations, and other more everyday mundane issues, the last four years have included a fill of momentous and traumatic events to keep him off kilter. These facts of life keep some of the important parts of his life on hold, including Amanda.

With the understanding that he does not intend to tell his wife about his crossdressing, Amanda recognizes that he may have dug a waist-deep hole that he will to stand in, indefinitely. Amanda understands that he may never find a perfect balance and that his life will continue on as it is as the status quo.

Suffering In Silence

So why does Amanda choose to live a segregated life, continually frustrated and missing out on a part of himself? For Amanda, the answer to that question comes easy – the risk is too great to do otherwise. Why reveal something that he feels will surely lead to him losing everything and everyone he cherishes.

Amanda has gone back and forth on the subject of telling Catherine about his feminine self, but cannot get over the belief and the fear that he will lose her and his boys. He is very analytical, constantly weighing the pros of sharing his full self with his wife versus the cons of losing it all.

He has done his own research on the subject, citing that behavioral psychology says that loss aversion plays a big factor in this case. The concept rings true for him, the endless probabilities swimming around his head in a fast riptide current. Thinking about the factors at play – his wife, his kids, potential fruits of professional success – leads to all of the aspects of his life that he deems more important than the sliver of self that represents his feminine self.

What if others found out? Amanda lives in fear that if other people in his family, his parents, aunts and uncles, cousins, found out about his crossdressing he would be branded with two scarlet letters on his chest – CD. In his mind, fear overwhelms any benefit he could think of about being honest with Catherine, diminishing the possibility that he could be Amanda in a more visible way.

So what is the downside of keeping the secret (besides keeping the secret)? Catherine has only seen her husband do manly things. She sees him watch sports, backpack in the woods, do yard work, and learn more about beer in the hopes of one day making his own brew. She will never truly understand that Amanda act of expressing his feminine side is what truly relaxes him. Since she has never seen ay of the feminine attributes of her husband, Catherine suggests manly pursuits as distractions and hobbies. This tends to lead to more frustration for him – not relief from it.

Because the social dynamic that Amanda and Catherine share with their neighbors is primarily focused around the wives and children, Amanda is faced with interacting with the other husbands. He finds these interactions forced, as he really has nothing in common with them other than the fact that they are all professionals.

As Amanda, he is more extroverted. He has common interests with other gurls. He can socialize with whom he wants, building relationships more naturally and organically. Plus, since crossdressers typically tend to bare their histories with each other, they do not operate with hidden agenda or expectation. Amanda prefers that sense of freedom when it comes to her friendships.

The Real World

Amanda wanted to reinforce that crossdressing (for him) is not real life or even a major component of his real world. His world is comprised of his career, his wife and his kids. Most times, Amanda has no place or position among those facets. As Amanda put it (and I am sure any parent can attest to), kids change everything. Everyone says it, but it cannot be overstated. The time and energy required for them makes one reassess how to approach life. It makes them work harder, smarter and better as a team (if possible).

Amanda and Catherine are working so hard and are so drained that, as a result, romance, intimacy and sex become afterthoughts. At times, Amanda feels like he has less of a wife and more of a really solid work partner and friend. It is something that Amanda knows he and Catherine needs to work on, but those days seem to be relegated to the future where the kids are older, in school full-time, and a bit less demanding of every life-giving second.

Amanda is also cordoned off to a future where there may be vague opportunities to emerge from his feminine cocoon. He claims that Catherine may not accept Amanda as part of their lives, but also states that she is very liberal and accepting of alternative social choices. She lets transsexuals and drag queens live and let live. She can understand these concepts. But there have been theoretical conversations about crossdressers that continue to give Amanda pause. Catherine has joked with friends and with Amanda that she just doesn't get why a *normal* man would want to wear a dress.

Risk Versus Reward

I asked Amanda what advice she has to offer to other crossdressers who are wrestling with revealing themselves to their partner. His answer was, "What advice can *they* offer me?" As with everything in life, opinions are like butt holes... everyone has one and they tend to stink. As Amanda tells it, every time he has a conversation with another crossdresser that swings around to this topic, the answer is typically; "You should tell her so you can be yourself." Amanda's answer is, "What if I'm risking huge parts of myself by telling her?"

For Amanda, she says that she would advise people to weigh the risks versus rewards – analyze the upside versus the downside – of sharing their crossdressing with their significant other. The upsides could include the relief of being completely honest with their partner, possibly more time being feminine, and maybe (just maybe) a partner who actively encourages and participates with them. The downsides are the loss of family, friends, children, professional status, and their standing in the community. They are risking the exposure of an irreversible *known*, understanding that their relationship will not be the same afterward.

Amanda advises that crossdressers need to look for clues from their spouses or partners as to how they would react to the knowledge, cautioning that even if the crossdresser is fairly certain of his partner's social position on the subject one never can predict the actual outcome. The most socially liberal and accepting person on the planet will not appreciate that their crossdressing partner has kept such an important part of them secret and hidden. The reveal of a crossdressing nature is a bombshell. But it will actually pale in comparison to the feelings of betrayal and trust that the partner will have.

Hope Isn't A Strategy

What kind of relationship does Amanda want between him and Catherine? He wants an open, accepting, and nurturing relationship. He wants them to bring out the best in one another, keep the romantic and intimate flames crackling, be each other' best friend, and allow for individual downtime to recharge.

Amanda is aware, that because of his crossdressing secret, he has chosen to inhibit many of the things he just outlined above. His fear of rejection and losing everything he holds dear stay his lips from sharing his secret. He is not willing to take the risk after having gone this far down this road.

He would love for Catherine and him to accidentally fall into the art of crossdressing. Amanda is looking for a narrative that would unravel like a fairytale where Catherine discovered that she loved it when her husband wore her panties and dresses. But as Amanda said, "… that's hope, and hope is not a strategy."

Regrets, I've Had A Few

Amanda says that he has two major regrets in his life. The first is his assumption that he needs to live up to other people's expectations; to be what others expect him to be. The second is not telling Catherine the whole truth about himself early on in the relationship.

Living with Crossdressing: Defining a New Normal

By his mid-twenties, Amanda was getting pressured by his traditional-minded family to get a wife, settle down, and have kids. Even with that familial coaxing, Amanda didn't have the heart to pursue a relationship. Finally, it was Catherine who pursued him. It was Catherine who made him realized that he was loved and worthwhile.

Amanda was adamantly against telling Catherine about his crossdressing. Why ruin a good thing? Plus, Amanda hadn't even understood that crossdressing was an integral part of him. He was in the early stages of acceptance at that point, just starting to think about getting a makeover and getting *her* out there.

If the time table had been moved forwards a year, the dynamic may have been different with telling Catherine. Amanda may have had more confidence in himself and with his female persona. He may have had less fear about revealing himself to the woman he loved. But at the time that they started dating, Amanda just wasn't there yet.

Amanda should have known better than to believe that his crossdressing was a phase or that those feelings would just go away, but he just pushed it to the back of his mind with the thought that he would deal with it later. That was a big mistake, because later is now, and he still hasn't dealt with his crossdressing as far as how it impacts their relationship.

The internal struggle and wrestling with the what-ifs of sharing the secret doesn't get any easier. Amanda is not sure that it ever will, but after a lot of thought and analysis, he has concluded that it is the best course of action (or non-action) for him – for now.

The New Gurl

> *Happiness is a butterfly, which when pursued, is always just beyond your grasp, but which, if you sit down quietly, may alight upon you.*
>
> ~ Nathaniel Hawthorne

> *There is nothing in a caterpillar that tells you it's going to be butterfly.*
>
> ~ R. Buckminster Fuller

Becoming

Nathaniel Hawthorne's quote of butterflies has nice similarities to many facets of the crossdressing life. From the obvious analogy of a butterfly emerging from a cocoon to striving to become something just beyond our grasp, all touch on the spirit of who and what we are.

Either as a youth or as an adult, all crossdressers have to come to terms with who they are. We can deny and fear our feminine emergence from the darkness of our minds for as long we deem fit but eventually we will have to stretch our wings and *become*. Otherwise, we face the risk of atrophy in some way – either in our relationship, our own balance, or in life.

I believe the more important point of the quote is that of the pursuit of the butterfly. You can't chase it. You have to have patience. Many crossdressers have lived with the slow development of their feminine personas over a period of years. We lifers have slowly become the New Girl, continuing to develop and perfect our personas as we go.

The late bloomers can have a different story. They have had to jumpstart their development over a period of months. Whether because of trauma, denial, or other emotional or environmental factors, many dressers don't find themselves facing a feminine mirror until later in their life. Their journey of self-discovery takes on a decidedly truncated development. There is urgency to it. There is a rush of regret for an undiscovered youth and for lost crossdressing opportunities. Now they are the New Girls.

The Pink Fog

While I am fairly certain that Jimmy Hendrix was very familiar with purple haze, I doubt he was versed in one of the pink variety. That may not be true, though, because my recent research has uncovered a Pink Haze strain of marijuana. But the pink haze I am referring to has a different meaning than *being so infatuated with someone that you can't think straight*. For the crossdresser, he is infatuated with someone, all right – *herself*! Hence, the pink fog (pink haze is for normal people infatuations) may have descended.

When the pink fog rolls in, it is a blinding and emotionally charged mist that encompasses a crossdresser's entire reason for being. Like having an addiction, the crossdresser in the pink fog can't get enough of their feminine forms, the charged excitement, and the untried adventures. Loved ones' feelings take a back seat to the crossdresser's desires. Every new adventure raises the bar of normalcy for the crossdresser while it scares the shit out of his partner.

How much is too much?

How fast is too fast?

How far is too far?

Each man's discovery of his femininity is different. Each relationship with their partner is unique. Each descent into the pink fog results in any measure of duration and degree of influence. Regardless, the most important takeaway is remembering its influence.

What do you mean?

Keep in mind how the experience affected you, and realize how it affected others. Remember, dear crossdresser, who you are. Don't lose those excellent qualities you possess in favor of paper-thin emotional highs. Don't forget that there is a woman (and possibly other family and children) who is struggling with this New Girl. You are not the only person in your own life (unless you are single and have zero attachments and commitments). You need to understand that everything you are reveling in and excited about is, mostly likely, unfamiliar to your significant other and holds nothing but trepidation.

Heck, I know that it's difficult to pass by every wig or pair of heels you see in the mall windows or online store. I have fallen prey to those urges, too. But with a limited budget, I don't have the luxury to buy whatever I want for Savannah. I get lucky with getting hand-me-downs from my girlfriend and finding great finds at garage sales. Some things can't be obtained through the cheap and thrifty methods, but that doesn't mean that you can't wear the same outfit in your closet more than once.

I'm On Top Of The World, Ma!

That is not what James Cagney is quoted as saying in *White Heat*. The actual quote is "Made it, Ma! Top of the world!". And so illustrates our memory and understanding of what is real and what is perceived. The point is that we can't always rely on memory when thinking that we have it all figured out. The moment you stop learning is the moment you stop living, said Tetsuyama-san.

So what are you talking about, Savannah?

Referring back to the Pink Fog, we crossdressers are not always in our right minds. Of course, that could be said about us in general terms, but please understand that a sudden rush of elation to the head after being given the green light to explore our femininity (typically within the relationship) is like skydiving for the first time.

The first time I crossed skydiving off my bucket list came with it several minutes of fear and questioning about whether this was the right idea (fear of talking about our crossdressing to our partner), followed by a sense of calm (the relief of sharing the secret), then more nervousness and fear for jumping out of a perfectly mechanically sound airplane (going out for the first time en femme), and finally taking the plunge and going into sensory overload.

Feminine sensory overload is the culprit that can stall your crossdressing acceptance by your partner. When you are freefalling, you feel like you are floating. I was so overwhelmed by my skydive and so focused on the other skydiver taking pictures and video of me that I completely missed out on the fact that I could have been taking in the curvature of the earth and witnessing the entirety of Long Island from 12,000 feet. Freedom to explore our crossdressing can possibly lead to such a ferocious single-mindedness of our femme selves that we fail to recognize the internal struggles of those around us. We may forget that they struggling with the idea that they are losing one of the best parts of themselves to a mistress – to this New Girl.

Masculinity vs Femininity

> *I definitely feel closer to the feminine side of the human being that I do the male – or the American idea of what a man is supposed to be. Just watch a beer commercial and you'll see what I mean.*
>
> ~ Kurt Cobain

> *Masculinity is not something given to you, but something you gain. And you gain it by winning small battles with honor.*
>
> ~ Norman Mailer

Medium

I heard a funny analogy that I thought would apply here. I told my co-workers that I paid for a psychic entertainment dinner package for Jen's birthday. And, yes, it was entertaining. One of my co-workers mentioned that there was a fundamental difference between magicians and psychics. Magicians are master of illusion while psychics and mediums claim to see the future and commune with the dead. Magicians are accepted without skepticism while most treat psychics with cynicism. There is a notion of implied trickery versus implied realism.

Can the same be true about crossdressers?

Do people see us and assume we are trying to trick people into believing we are women? Knowing that many of us will be "clocked" as men while out dressed as our feminine selves, is that really a concern? I have heard stories where men at bars will be frustrated and angry when finding out that they were attracted to a woman who ended up having 'a little something extra'.

They feel cheated and deceived, that they were baited into their attraction to the crossdresser, uncertain as to why they were caught in the allure to that fake woman sipping an apple martini at the bar. That uncertainty may lead to strange feelings that those men will not understand how to process.

And like men do, they will probably lash out in some way.

Typical men!

But is it typical?

Gender Stereotypes

We have been conditioned from birth (practically) to accept men and women as having certain traits. Boys are designated as blue (sometimes yellow) and girls are designated as pink. I mean, how would we be able to know the sex of the baby at the gender reveal party if we didn't know what color to use?

I understand that, in general, men have more muscle mass and women are more maternal, and...um... I actually had to go to the vast and deep knowledge of the Internet to recall the actual stereotypes (since I ain't one). According to PlannedParenthood.org, there are four basic kinds of gender stereotypes; personality traits, domestic behaviors, occupations, and physical appearance.

The first, personality traits, relegates woman to the more passive and submissive roles, while men are expected to be more self-confident and aggressive. Men are hunter... women are gatherers. Men club women on their heads and drag them by the hair back to their caves.

The second trait, domestic behaviors, revolves around the dynamic of the division of labor within a nuclear relationship. Women are maternal (see, I remembered one!), best suited for the caring and raising of the children. Men, on the other hand, are expected to be able to fix a pipe and mow the lawn. How long will a wife or girlfriend fume at the overflowing kitchen garbage because it is the man's job to tie up the bag and take it to the can outside? How often will men wait for their spouses to prepare dinner for them?

When it comes to occupations, the third stereotype of the gender split still persists. It reminds me of the following riddle:

> *A father and son are in a horrible car crash that kills the dad. The son is rushed to the hospital; just as he's about to go under the knife, the surgeon says, "I can't operate—that boy is my son!"*
> *Explain.*

Did you get the right answer?
Did it take you a minute?
Give up?

The person couldn't operate on the boy because it was the boy's mother. Wait! What? The doctor was a female surgeon? Preposterous!

That is a standard of occupational stereotyping that we have had engrained in us from an early age. It is based on classifying woman as second-class citizens with the assumption that women lacked the intelligence to pursue male-dominated careers. We couldn't fathom that women just weren't afforded the opportunity to get the education necessary for those jobs. Instead, we just thought they were being dumb ole girls. And then the opposite is still kind of true. Men in female-dominated roles – secretaries, executive assistants, nurses – are considered to be *less than* and made as the butt of jokes about doing a woman's job. Luckily, that dynamic is slowly changing.

The last, and probably the most apropos to our discussions, is physical appearance. Men are expected to be broad-shouldered, tall, and muscular. Women are expected to be graceful and small, slight of frame, and demure. If you sit in a Starbucks for any period of time and people watch (like I do while I am writing), you will see a myriad of people in all shapes, sizes, and colors. But we still cling to popularized and standardized notions of what women and men should be and how they should conduct themselves.

Words commonly used to describe femininity are:

dependent	weak
emotional	flirtatious
passive	nurturing
sensitive	self-critical
quiet	soft
graceful	sexually submissive
innocent	accepting

Words commonly used to describe masculinity are:

independent	competitive
non-emotional	clumsy
aggressive	experienced
tough-skinned	strong
active	sexually aggressive
self-confident	rebellious
hard	

These traits are very back-and-white. There is no flexibility to allow or accept masculinity within the feminine list, and visa versa. All men and women – all humans – are an amalgam of both lists, with some traits more dominant in their lives than others.

The hope is to accept people for who they are regardless of the mix of the recipe. Maybe if we were more open-minded about others, they would not feel the need to suppress their identities. And this belief carries way beyond the spectrum of crossdressers.

Gender Beginnings

There is a feeling of condemnation that some people experience when a crossdressing partner reveals his femininity. The crossdresser has now destroyed the gender lines in the relationship. The biological boundary, once an established and stable *constant*, is forever altered.

Thanks, crossdressing partner, the spouse says with pointed sarcasm.

All of a sudden, the revelation explains so much as to why her man is the way he is! Everything makes perfect sense now as to why he was sometimes withdrawn and depressed. Now the spouse realizes why her man is so interested in her fashion and is able to provide that rare insight for what looks best on her and why he crosses his legs the way he does, or why he is so touchy-feely.

Why can't men cry when they watch *The Green Mile*? That scene at the warden's house is heartbreaking. So is the scene when John Coffey shakes Paul Edgecomb's hand before riding the lightning... sniff. Why are men expected to express their feelings differently than women? Have we been so conditioned in our gender roles that the mere notion of impropriety of our specific and defined gender will condemn us in the eyes of others?

We are conditioned.

From birth we are shown what it means to be a boy or a girl. Many younger couples are employing a more relaxed parenting concept, nurturing their children with more encouragement than with defined structure and restrictions. When I grew up, parents still adhered to the traditional gender norms. I would have been petrified if my dad found out that I liked to dress in frilly and satiny clothes. I knew inherently that what I was doing would not be accepted. I had been conditioned with what appropriate gender roles were for girls and for boys, the gender lines established in my brain by the family dynamic, my socialization with other kids, and what I saw on television. Hey, I loved Sesame Street, but don't ever remember seeing any of those boy Muppets wearing pink.

I loved Grover and Cookie Monster.

That being said, did you know that Sesame Street has recently introduced its own relevant segment about gender expression called the Dress-Up Me Club? In the segments, Abby Cadabby plays with her pals, Prairie Dawn and Elmo, and decides they will all be superheroes or princesses. Abby is told that superhero-ing is for boys and playing princess is for girls. These lovable furry monsters soon discover that it doesn't matter whether you are a boy or girl to express who you want to be.

In the last couple years retailers like Toys R Us and Target have begun to phase out the labeling of their toys being geared toward "boys" or "girls". Thanks to input by parents and progressives, marketing had been remodeled to focus on the encouragement of the child's creativity and development, not the one-dimensional gender baseline of aggressive masculine behavior for boys and domestic service for girls. It is a positive shift in thinking, but it is just a start since those mixed toy aisles are still filled with pink Barbie and Littlest Pet Shop packaging versus techy sci-fi LEGO or NERF boxes (although NERF has come out with their girl-demographic Rebelle line of foam dart weapons).

It Begins With The Truth

It's great that boys and girl are starting to be deprogrammed from the traditional gender roles. Spectacular! But what about all the thirty-something and above men and women who have already been conditioned with what they understand gender to be? For them (and I mean me, too), it will always be an uphill battle to win over hearts and minds about how us crossdressers are actually a normally occurring phenomenon.

As I had mentioned earlier, I knew well enough to hide my crossdressing from my mother's disapproval and my father's wrath. That fear served to lock me into a veneer of an accepted masculine role in order to conform. It has taken years to deprogram myself as to what is the truth for me.

We all have a desire to be true to ourselves (as far as we understand the truth to be). Social norms have and will influence how far we deny our authentic self. Why explore something within ourselves that is considered abhorrent and subject to scorn and ridicule?

No human enjoys rejection.

None of us want to fear for our safeties.

All of us strive to be loved and accepted.

So many of us *go along to get along*, taking on the mantles of exaggerated masculinity in order to be accepted. Play sports in high school, pursue girls like all hormone-crazed boys do, get a manly job, act tough and debase others to elevate ourselves… you know, all of those typical things people do. These concepts serve to mentally castrate the crossdressing man (ouch) from his innate feminine feelings.

In fact, all men have what would be defined as feminine feelings, not just crossdressing and homosexual ones. Women have masculine feelings. We only label them because we all need labels for things. Yes, stereotypes have their roots in truth, but stereotypes are the simplest form of a definition of any group. Asians are all smart. Caucasians are all privileged. African Americans are all thugs. Crossdressers are all sex-crazed perverts. We perpetuate the myths based on a vague understanding of the group as a whole. Worse, we cling to those generalities in our ignorance, validating every experience where it reinforces our existing bias and ignoring all other proof that runs contrary to our existing beliefs.

Crossdressers Are Dumb

Conversely (not the shoe, but an important sounding word), crossdressers are guilty of using pre-defined female stereotypes to define our own feminine identities. And, not only that, we can exaggerate the female form to such a degree in our pursuit of our presentation of womanhood that we fail to realize that we are close to becoming a parody of that which we hold in the highest regard. It's a crazy rollercoaster loopty-loop of double standards.

Women can wear pants, but men can't wear skirts. Women can be masculine and assertive for their careers, but men are teased for having feelings (although women are still considered to be the B-Word sometimes if too assertive, unfortunately). Women are applauded for being more like men. Men are ridiculed or labeled as gay if they seem more effeminate.

Sigh.

A crossdresser's feminine pursuit can put him on a collision course of epitomizing an outdated cookie-cutter version of what he believes the perfect woman to be. I have met several gurls who love the now trendy retro look, happy to take on a 1950s pearl-adorned housewife persona.

Is that what they think a woman is?

Isn't that more of a masquerade than an expression?

Who am I to judge what their gender expression is?

I am also guilty of taking my feminine expression to a level beyond where some cis-women do (even on their best dress up days). I prefer heels that are 3 inches or higher. I love form-fitting dresses and outfits that can accentuate my fake curves, even if going to a casual restaurant. I love heavier smoky eye makeup and thick lashes. Oh, and I must have French manicure press-on nails.

Do I over-sexualize the female form?

Probably.

Most women will cast away those high heels under the reception hall table in favor of uncrushed toes and distressed arches. We crossdressers will keep those heels on all night. We wear corsets tight enough to leave indentations in our torsos at the end of the night. We suffer for our craft. We endure the pain and discomfort for the illusion of our expression. Anything less and we will feel incomplete.

My girlfriend has been great with giving me constructive criticism and offering me her now too-big clothes. She has a spirited, gypsy style and I have been happy to add these items into my wardrobe. What we constantly disagree on is the tightness and length of the hemline of my skirts. Can't agree on everything, I guess. And I can't make the general populace suffer by covering up my best assets – my legs!

Some crossdressers need to re-evaluate their feminine expression to be more modern and trendy if they wish to become *one of the girls*. If the goal is to blend in, there are fashion trends and parameters that are in place in certain locales that are acceptable. Keeping to these guidelines will allow you to ghost through a restaurant without turning heads (in a negative appraising way). Five inch heeled thigh high boots may not be the best choice for a run to Starbucks.

As the knight guarding the Holy Grail in the cave said in the final act of *Indiana Jones and the Last Crusade*, choose wisely.

True To Form

An important thing to keep in mind is the idea that you have to be balanced and be true to who you are. We all have both a masculine and feminine side. The only reason why the two halves are separated is because we have been taught that they are to be separated. Corralling appropriate gender behavior has been based on a system of social restrictions set in place long before we stepped into it.

For me, I have always known that I saw the world a bit differently than the other boys around me. I wasn't good at sports, although I tried to fit in on the varsity squad. I didn't care for the roughhousing and stupidity that other boys immersed themselves in throughout their adolescence. I had more female friends than those of my own gender. I focused on school, and eventually, girlfriends, then college and life beyond that. I thought I was an old soul because I wasn't into all of the hi-jinks that I witnessed around me.

So I tried to be more like everyone else. I don't think I really went out of my way on a conscious level, though. I mean, I liked playing on the high school football team, although I didn't appreciate the testosterone-fueled aggressiveness off the field. Boys are dumb that way. I was more of a bookworm, a nerd, a geek... you know, all those other labels we have thrust upon us.

I believe that my lack of machismo allowed me to be more in balance with who I truly am. And that is the natural byproduct of the most important quality we can bring to ourselves and to others. Honesty.

We have to be true to ourselves. As crossdressers, it is of the utmost importance to explore all we can about who we could possibly be. There isn't a crossdressing manual to refer to, except the vast cross-functional reading that is available on the Internet. Let me remind you that I'm talking about much more than erotic fiction and webcam sites.

Be thoughtful.

Be mindful.

Be reflective.

Only through the rigors of a thorough self-examination will you discover what you have been suppressing. I'm not talking about the Pink Fog that so many crossdressers will blast through in an effort to make up for lost time, but looking into your soul to discover what is hidden there. Armed with the maps and journals of that exploration will allow you to more easily open a dialogue with your partner.

There will be hard questions asked of you. They are important questions that need to be discussed, with no hesitation or worries about what the answer may be. If you don't know the answers or are afraid of the answers, dear crossdressers, do not get defensive or adamant about your position on the subject. Allow the conversation to unravel as you both travel this road together.

Half Cocked Or Full Bore

I know the things I'm saying sound daunting.

They are daunting. But they are not insurmountable or herculean tasks. Revealing yourself to your partner is not the only step you need to take together. It is the first utterance in a lifetime of discussions, turmoil, tears, and joy as you navigate these waters together.

Living with Crossdressing: Defining a New Normal

Crossdressers, you need to understand who you truly are and what your needs are. Your partners deserve nothing less. Dear partners, you need to ask questions, read books, and find others in the same position. In the meanwhile, try not to judge your crossdressing man too harshly based on what you *think* a crossdresser represents.

Crossdressers, try to stay away from the Pink Fog. Just because you have talked to your partner about who you are, you need to step with caution as you move forward. Just because your partner has not thrown you out of the house doesn't mean that every day is a feminine Mardi Gras.

Be sure, dear crossdressers, to appreciate your partner. Show her gratitude for sticking with you and wanting to better understand you. Show her that you are still masculine in the ways that she fell in love with. Yeah, that could be an innuendo if you want to think that way. Remember that your spouse was attracted to a man. And, dear partner, remember you fell in love with someone with intangible qualities that set him apart from the other men you had previously associated with. Perhaps now they make better sense to you.

Somewhere in the above paragraph is the balance. Crossdressers need to be true to each side of their gender identity, keeping in mind that the person that loves them the most is not ready to forego the man they love for the woman you want them to love.

But I'm the same person either way.

That may be true, dear crossdresser, but you are still presenting as someone that your partner is not familiar with.

Make love to a woman... wait, now I'm a lesbian?

Hold hands with a stranger... hey, I don't know you, lady!

You're the same man underneath... that's not what those stockings and corset say to me!

Prove to your spouse that you are the same person regardless of your gender expression.

Are you less kind as a woman? Why?

Are you more flirtatious? How come?

nope Are you attracted to men when you dress as a woman? Is that because you want to have sex with them or because you love the attention?

These are basic questions that crossdressers need to ask themselves, and partners have every right to ask. Understanding why we do things when we are dressed shouldn't be a mystery to us. If they are, then that mystery will become something that your partner will be desperate to solve, even if she needs to make a number of assumptions based on her own level of knowledge and experience to do so.

What's That Expression?

The non-fetish, non-transitioning crossdresser doesn't want to be locked into one gender expression. For one, I love being a genetic man as much as I love dressing to the nines as Savannah. I don't mind a bit of scruff (until it gets itchy). I also don't mind a tight bodycon scuba dress (on me or my girlfriend).

I don't dress to attract men, although I admit it's flattering when they want to buy me a drink. It's a cliché but it's a validation of the gender expression I'm exhibiting at that moment. Savannah would be just as flattered if a woman did the same.

We all want to be appreciated and loved. These social conventions serve to support the notion that we are attractive,

Living with Crossdressing: Defining a New Normal

desirable, and accepted. A typical crossdresser does not dress to go on the prowl for a man, nor do they dress as a woman to mock her femininity. Crossdressers find relief from the typical masculine via donning feminine attire and applying makeup. This allows them to express themselves in a manner that is typically reserved for the female of our species.

I remember going into The Village in NYC on Halloween dressed as my favorite female Marvel superhero. A man came up to me and asked me for a light for his cigarette. If you saw me, you would know there was no place on my person to hide any flammable materials. Below is the exchange, verbatim:

"Do you have a light?"
"Sorry," I said in my male voice. "I don't smoke."
"Oh, shit. You're a dude!" he replied and drifted away.

I was flattered that this young drunk man didn't clock me as a man until I spoke. I felt good about myself and how I was able to pass casual inspection presenting as a woman. I felt sexy and desirable. Later on that night, several young female Asian tourists stopped me to take a smart phone group picture. They made me feel just as good as the guy had earlier. I was happy that I could be a good memory of their Halloween night in New York City.

Do you want to be perceived as a woman?

I have to say I don't know. I would love to be passable as a woman when I decide to do so. I have no problem using the men's room in a restaurant if dressed as a woman, because that is how I regard myself (a man, in general). I do struggle with wanting to perfect my feminine appearance and wish that some of the curves and tone were naturally more female at those times so I could shed the use of padding and wear more revealing outfits.

There is an inherent convention that gender dictates sexuality. Men are attracted to women, and women are attracted to men. That is the normal species default but it's not an absolute. Many alternative sexual lifestyles are at play throughout society and the world. Regardless of who you are attracted to, someone in that form will be appealing to you. Therefore, it is assumptive to think that if you are presenting as that gender you must be attracted to the opposite gender. It's funny that, as I wrote that last sentence, I was tempted to write "...must be attracted to the opposite sex..."

We do need to be more mindful that gender expression is not equal to our sexual orientation. Most crossdressers would like to experience their female sides with their girlfriends or wives. That way they would feel that their partners loved them as a whole person, even if the expression is halved.

Body Image

I'm going to soapbox for a moment.

Fair warning!

Dear partners, please realize that we crossdressers put so much effort into our female presentation because 1) we have to in order to simulate anything close to femininity, 2) we want our appearance to be flawless, 3) we don't want to be "clocked" by other men and women, and 4) we are doing our damnedest to emulate the female ideal that we have set on the highest pedestal.

In our interviews, we have come across women who have become part of their crossdresser partner's journey. More often than not, the cis-woman is intimidated by the effort that their crossdressing mate puts into his process to get ready. The woman may suffer from self-esteem issues as a result of the fact that they don't put on heels and foundation every time they decide to leave the house to go to the grocery store for milk, bread and eggs.

Have they become complacent?

Have they lost a bit of the luster from their own sensuality and femininity?

For me, I envy women for being women. They have all of the assets that they need. We crossdressers have to put hours in while our girlfriends or wives can put in practiced minutes to get ready to go out on the town. I am always an advocate that we should strive to be the best we can be, physically and mentally. Each of us, men and women, should celebrate our body and the effort we put into it. We are all beautiful creatures. Sometimes we just have to be reminded of that fact.

Passing Thoughts

Crossdressing is typically not a passing fancy. It may be something that men fight against and suppress throughout their lives. We may try, time after time, to purge the urge out of our systems, only to find that the desire comes back to haunt us. Living in denial was only good for Queen Cleopatra.

Once we understand that our personal expression of crossdressing is not a fetish or a phase, the next step is to understand and fully accept ourselves. That will allow others to accept us – through the confidence we exude, education, enlightenment, and being a beacon of truth and a positive example for others to find and follow.

We try so hard to emulate and blend in as women that sometimes we forget that passability is not the same as acceptance. Hell, tolerance is not the same as acceptance! Being mistaken for a woman at first glance is not the same as being accepted as a crossdresser. My writing of this book is my attempt to go beyond my abilities to pass as a woman and get into the unknown territories of acceptance of which we are – crossdressers.

Have You Heard That Joke?

> *My mission in life is not merely to survive but to thrive; and to do so with some passion, some compassion, some humor, and some style.*
>
> ~ Maya Angelou

> *Everything is funny, as long as it's happening to somebody else.*
>
> ~ Will Rogers

Truth In Life

I have a wonderful friend named Lisa who adores the fact that I have an alternative gender identity. When I first told her, she was excited and interested, and best of all, totally accepting. Jen and I met Lisa and her fiancé for coffee and dessert at a local coffee shop. Lisa gushed about how awesome it was to have me as a friend, adamant with her love and support of me.

After we said our goodbyes and made our way to our car, Jen made the point that it's easier for Lisa to be objective when she doesn't have to live with a crossdresser. Jen, in those days, was still a bit shell-shocked as she tried to find her bearings on handling what was happening between the three of us (counting Savannah).

Jen is right, though. While Lisa had been exposed to folks with different sexual orientations and gender identities, Jen had never been close to such people and grew up with a more traditional gender perspective of men and women.

Additionally, before I revealed Savannah, Jen had admitted that an early boyfriend had surprised her by dressing in lingerie. The reveal was quick, awkward and embarrassing. Jen mentioned that she may have cursed with surprise and left the house, hoping normalcy would resume upon her return.

Two Crossdressers Walk Into A Bar

Let's take a break from all of the information and stories you are consuming and committing to memory with perfect clarity, accuracy, and understanding. I offer you a silly, and somewhat true, list of reasons why it's better to be in a loving relationship with a crossdresser.

I know that many (if not most) women want their mates to be burly, macho and manly. It goes without saying since the majority of pairings between a man and a woman follow these conventions. But I am here to break the stranglehold of these social constructs, not because they are wrong, but because there is room for other definitions of what makes a relationship functional and successful.

This list is for the women who love their men just the way they are. They love both the amalgam of the masculinity and the femininity that their partners possess. Women, do your men dote on you and consider you a porcelain sculpture deserving of nothing less than a pedestal? Are they loving and understanding in a way that is a bit different than your other previous boyfriends (or… gasp… husbands)? If you loved the totality of your men's personality prior to you finding out that they loved to wear feminine clothes, this Top 35 list is for you!

The List

1. Your crossdresser is more in tune with the female mind. Men generally try to *fix things*. Your partner will be more apt to talk out issues and won't devalue your feelings.
2. Your crossdresser will be more apt to like chick flicks, and won't be embarrassed to be seen at the theater with you.
3. Your crossdresser is more emotional, cries easily at the movies, and melts over puppies and kittens.
4. Your crossdresser is happy to take you out on the dance floor, regardless of how good they think they can dance.
5. Your crossdresser is fiercely loyal to you, and recognizes how wonderful you are.
6. Your crossdresser can keep a secret. They have had plenty of practice.
7. Your crossdresser is open to the idea of consulting a therapist to better your relationship – and him.
8. You have a valuable fashion consultant who knows what you look best in. Gone are the days of hearing your man say, "It looks fine".
9. If you are close to the same sizes, you have now effectively doubled your wardrobe. Plus, you can experiment with a style that may not necessarily be what you think will work.
10. Your crossdresser will always be envious of what you are wearing, knowing that if you both wore the same outfit you will always Wear It Best!
11. Your crossdresser will always be up for a day of clothes shopping with you (see #8 above, again!).

12. You have a girlfriend as well as a boyfriend. Your crossdresser will be your closest and most intimate friend in all ways, if you want him to be.
13. Want to change your own look? Just grab an outfit out of your crossdresser's closet and a wig off the stand and be whoever you want to be.
14. Your crossdresser will be forever grateful that you take an interest in how he should appropriately apply makeup. And he can show you tips you weren't ever aware of. Thank you, YouTube tutorials!
15. Your crossdresser will be sympathetic about how you feel about your hairy legs.
16. Your crossdresser will never be irritated that you need another 15 minutes to get ready for an engagement. He knows what effort it takes to feel beautiful and presentable.
17. Don't have a body briefer? Put a run in your last pair of pantyhose? No problem. Your crossdresser has got you covered.
18. Your crossdresser appreciates your body, style and mind.
19. If you buy something for the home, your crossdresser will never have an issue with it being too girly.
20. The toilet seat will always be down. No more midnight ass splashdowns!
21. Your crossdresser understands and empathizes with how you might feel about your body. He has battled a poor body image for years!
22. Your crossdresser will join you at the nail or beauty salon with no complaints.
23. Your crossdresser knows how to do the laundry – the right way!

Living with Crossdressing: Defining a New Normal

24. Your crossdresser has walked a mile in your shoes – literally.
25. Your crossdresser treats a lady like a lady should be treated.
26. Your crossdresser loves to engage in deeper, longer... you guessed it... conversation.
27. Remember what you were thinking for #26? Your crossdresser loves that, too.
28. Your crossdresser would love to experiment in the bedroom with whatever you come up with. Plus, you get a girlfriend, if that is something of interest.
29. Your crossdresser is always attentive to making sure you look your best.
30. Your crossdresser's gurlfriends will all love you. Do you know why? Because you are awesome!
31. Your crossdresser loves to snuggle more than you do.
32. Your crossdresser puts your needs first.
33. Don't have the right shade of makeup or lipstick? Odds are your crossdresser does!
34. Your crossdresser loves to show you affection at any time, regardless of how they are dressed.
35. Even though your crossdresser knows how to keep a secret, they are genuine with their critiques (food, fashion, style, etc.). They want to know what works and what don't work, and will do the same for you.

BONUS

36. No macho bullshit. You get all the feminine qualities without the competitiveness and cattiness that sometimes comes along with it.

From Closet To Coatrack

Love makes your soul crawl out from its hiding place.
  ~ Zora Neale Hurston

I went to the woods because I wished to live deliberately, to front only the essential facts of life, and see if I could not learn what it had to teach, and not, when I came to die, discover that I had not lived.
  ~ Henry David Thoreau

Living In Darkness

Many crossdressers have lived in darkness and with secrecy for much of their lives. As lifetime dressers, they were faced with the inherent knowledge that what they did wasn't acceptable. Personally, I never felt shame for the act of dressing. However, I did have shame for trespassing where I wasn't supposed to be and for the thought that others would shun me for who I was. The inferences from television and the comments from those closest to me trained me to believe that I was something unnatural and uncommon. It wasn't until a move to NYC and the growing popularity of the Internet did I realize that I wasn't just a feminine fetish freak. Others, those late bloomers, may have lived with deep-rooted denials of who they were, having suppressed a vague notion based on a misunderstanding and fear of their attraction to female attire.

Whatever the reasons, crossdressers have lived in the shadows of one fear or another. Now, you are faced with a brand new social circumstance where you must understand how to dig out from that pit to emerge into the world. The first step, the most shocking and painful step on both sides, is dealing with the telling. Imagine a man who holds a secret so long that they can't fathom how to utter the words and can't rationalize a positive outcome. Some secrets are best kept secrets, in our skewed opinion. Better to perpetuate it, stacking fibs, white lies, and bald-faced deceit to the mix until the web we have created is too sticky and tight to escape.

Keep It In Context

Sir Walter Scott wrote, *Oh! What a tangled web we weave, when first we practice to deceive.* In the Bible, John 8:32 reads as, *And ye shall know truth, and the truth shall make you free.* One references a love triangle in a play and the other teaches about an understanding of a higher power. What both represent to me in this context is that telling truth is easier than lies. Honesty is better than deceit. I am not advocating an admission in all cases or with all partners. That is a decision that only you can make for yourself. But if you are reading this book, dear reader, you may have already been exposed to the scary truth of speaking it or hearing it, or on the cusp of sharing your authentic self.

Where do we go from here? Can we adapt? Can we accept each other in this new dynamic? There are so many questions with so many answers. And, all that I can guarantee is that none of the answers will come easy. The answers will lead to more questions… and more answers… and on and on.

But let's assume, dear partner, that you have taken the first steps. Let's assume that by reading this book you are open to expanding your understanding of what makes your crossdressing partner tick. You may find your situation uncertain and scary, but you are obviously taking a good step by reading my effort. I am sure you are also devouring other books, articles, and blogs that offer a measure of enlightenment. As we have discussed, though, knowledge comes with its own challenges.

Conversation, Not Confrontation

Take a few minutes, a few days, or longer to get composed, armed with your new knowledge. Take a series of deep breaths and sit down with your crossdressing partner with your questions.

Beloved partners, set ground rules if you feel that your crossdresser may be overly sensitive, tense or averse to questioning. Re-affirm that you love him and remind him that this is a safe space to discuss whatever has come to mind from the reading. Remember that your crossdressing partner is in just as raw an emotional state as you. His fears of rejection and of your judgment abound. Be objective in your questions, mindful of his responses, and caring in your follow-ups.

Crossdressers, remember that questions asked are not a direct attack on you, just an attempt to understand where your crossdressing fits into the fabric of the gender spectrum and your relationship. Understand that your partner has little practical experience with anyone with your gender identity, while you have had plenty of time to come to terms with it.

Be patient and honest. You may find that the questions you answer will give you an even higher enlightenment of yourself, too. Listen to your partner... hear her words. Do not tack on your own fears and assumptions to her queries.

Also remember that this is not a sprint, but a marathon. The same questions may be re-asked over several sit-downs (you know, like the mafia). Understanding does not come with one response. It also doesn't necessarily come with several responses. It sometimes doesn't even come through with words at all.

One of Jen's favorite sayings from me is, "Show, don't tell."

When she worried about what Savannah was really about, I didn't continue to try to persuade her with more talk. I truly took that phrase to heart and continued to demonstrate my commitment to her, to our relationship, and to elevating what Savannah was for us.

Actions speak volumes louder than the most vocal and eloquent of speeches. Words are meaningless and hollow without actions. They are fragile and frail, their promise broken sometimes with the simplest notions of impropriety. If you have hope that your new dynamic will survive and thrive, your partner needs to see that what you say is what you do.

Trust Falls

In business and in life, there are several suggestions that will help in trust building. Crossdressers, the following may help you during this tenuous time in your relationship.

1. Do what you say you're going to. Your promises must equal your actions.
2. Be consistent. As with anything, stability and continuity help to keep the mind at ease.

3. Listen. Make sure your partner feels heard. Try to understand her perspective before answering with your own.
4. When she makes a statement or has a question, first repeat back to her what you understand her to mean. A measure of clarity will save a lot of angst and unnecessary miscommunication.
5. Be direct. Don't beat around the bush. Don't dodge questions thrown at you.
6. Be caring. Give of yourself and sacrifice for your partner. Understand that her support of your crossdressing is (initially) a major sacrifice for what she understands her way of life to be.
7. Do the right thing. Talking about your crossdressing is an opportunity to better understand each other and yourself.
8. Be vulnerable. Opening yourself up to your partner shows that you are sincere in your efforts to be trustworthy.

Space Allocations

The hope of all crossdressers is to have a full existence with the woman they love. To be accepted (to whatever degree is comfortable for both of you) is to be loved. In my case, I would love for Jen to see *me* under it all and not even distinguish a difference based on the clothes I wear or the make-up I apply. I love her with all of my heart and hope that she can love both of me with all of her heart. Of course, there is a defined difference between male and female personas, but I am still me under it.

For our relationship, we continue to be a work in progress. Sometimes I need to check myself and my expectations for what I want, focusing instead on acknowledging and feeling gratitude for our lives together at this moment. My word of advice is to always keep your head where your feet are, otherwise you find your mind dwelling in the mires of the past or staring at the unrealized expectations of the future.

In the here and now, Jen and I share clothes and makeup, she comes with me to private events and casual dinners with my gurlfriends (some of them with their own significant others). She sacrificed two of our apartment's three closets to accommodate both my male side and Savannah. I would like to think she has access to anything in Savannah's closet, so I consider it an even 50/50 split!

She still disagrees about the amount of body hair I have (I want less, she wants more – or at least for it to not be prickly on her skin. Gross!). We still try to be discrete when we leave the apartment, if only to keep the level of drama to a minimum.

There is comfort in having a measure of control over a situation when there seems to be a shortage of it. As a couple, it is important to keep a set of agreed upon rules in place for yourselves and others. It helps to keep disappointment low and expectations in perspective. It also helps to keep you focused in the here and now, understanding where the boundaries are, and allowing for the mind to be freed up for the spontaneity of the present.

It seems counterintuitive.

I agree that it does sound incorrect. But let me illustrate with a personal anecdote. I want so much for Jen to interact with me as Savannah just like she does with my male persona. I love to kiss and hug Jen whenever the feeling strikes. When I am dressed as Savannah, that feeling doesn't just go away. She is still the woman I love.

Living with Crossdressing: Defining a New Normal

One evening while we were out at an event, I spent much of the night calculating whether it would be okay to touch her leg or give her a hug or a kiss on the cheek. I was so wrapped up in that internal debate that I missed out on having gratitude that she was out with me in the first place. My mood was soured and I did nothing as a result to make Jen more comfortable with the experience.

Crossdressers, when your partners make room in their closets, remember that they are not just providing you more square footage in your home but are also giving you real estate in their heads and hearts. Do not make the extra space heavier with clutter than it needs to be for her – or you.

Be in the moment.

Be there for each other.

Crossdressers, please try to understand your partner's point of view. It should be easy since we claim that we are more in tune with women than the average male.

The Purge

Life is a great big canvas; throw all the paint you can at it.
~ Danny Kaye

Throw off your worries when you throw off your clothes at night.
~ Napoleon Bonaparte

Expensive Proposition

Many men have gone through The Purge, that expensive and most-times futile attempt to be rid of *the sickness* that is crossdressing. By getting rid of the clothes that entice them to trade their masculinity with femininity, they hope for a fresh start at the gender they are born as. There are many reasons why crossdressers go through this process.

The first is that they feel in their hearts that they are sick. They do what any addict would do to kick the habit. Get rid of the offending things that enable the illness. Go cold turkey. Donate the clothes, heels, and wigs. Throw it all in a dumpster. Stay away from sites with crossdressing pictures and erotica. Re-invest in more masculine pursuits. Be more of a man!

Associated with the above, another reason is being caught by a shocked and angry spouse. In these cases, there is no talking it out or attempting to understand the compulsions of why they dress. It is a torrid affair. There is mistrust and an unwillingness to understand. Then comes the ultimatum. Choose the partner or the dressing. The crossdresser, with fear of losing all he holds dear, gets rid of everything that serves as a reminder of his femme self.

Some crossdressing men simply lose interest in dressing up. The urge to don their feminine attire fades and the clothes just sit around in boxes or storage. It may seem a waste to hold on to these articles and they are eventually given or thrown away. There is nothing sinister about the decisions. They are usually the result of space allocation and practicality.

The best form of purging is that of keeping up with current trends and good appearances. Unless you are rocking some in-style retro styles, it is best to leave the parachute pants and big hairdos to the 80s. Clothing get threadbare and torn, heels get scuffed and broken, and wigs get ratty and frayed. It is smart to keep up with current fashion as best you can. Remember that those old styles will come back around but in modified ways. I believe that staying a bit modern does offer a measure of passibility for you and normalcy for your partner.

I Am Not An Animal!

As you have read above, I referred to crossdressing as a sickness. I do NOT share that as one of my reasons for why I want to dress as a woman. I do not believe I have an illness or addictive compulsion to become Savannah. There was no trauma in my childhood that would shape me to want to escape into femininity. I am just me. And for me, that is reason enough.

Also, I do not hold to any modern religious conventions that my crossdressing is an abomination to the will of God. According to the church, I am debasing myself and focusing on my own wants and desires versus giving myself over to Jesus and to God. I cannot give myself over to a deity that in the same breath offers compassion to all, but condemnation to those he and the Bible scribes as undesirable.

Alternative sexual orientation has become a non-issue and accepted among metropolitan and modern-thinking people. Does that mean that the church should continue to lead the charge against them? So many religious groups preach intolerance under the guise of love for all. The flavor of hypocrisy leaves a very bitter taste on my tongue.

For the non-fetish, non-transitioning crossdresser, our feminine and masculine sides are just part of our overall persona. We don't go out to hurt anyone. We only want to live a normal life.

What Is Normal?

> *In many countries today, moral and ethical norms are being reconsidered; national traditions, differences in nation and culture are being erased.*
> ~ Vladimir Putin

> *The very ink with which history is written is merely fluid prejudice.*
> ~ Mark Twain

Forced Perspective

I'm a hypocrite… pure and simple.

I believe myself to be a normal individual in every way. Even my desire to dress as a woman feels normal to me. And why wouldn't it feel as normal as the sound of my breathing or the rhythm of my heartbeat? My want to dress emerged years before any adolescent sexuality had made crossdressing a reward reinforced behavior. And, of course, I am going to side with me on matters such as these.

I'm not as cavalier as I may have been in my misspent youth, choosing to spend this period of my life reflecting on the whys and why not's of my existence and of my feminine side. I am more aware of how it affects others, especially the *normal* people. There was a time when I had a sense of entitlement about Savannah, but now I strive to strike balance in my life about all things – my work, my relationship, my passions and, yes, my crossdressing.

We all possess a perspective shaped by our own beliefs, environment, and experiences. Not everyone enjoys the same television programs, movies or sporting events. Some people don't enjoy sports at all! No one takes away the same enlightenment from reading poetry or gets the same raw emotion from a painting hung in a gallery. There are hundreds of music genres and plenty of ears to enjoy each melody.

And while we each like what we like, we don't necessarily care for what others like. We shouldn't hold malice for each other's tastes and preferences. Of course, that is not true when it comes to what our parents and grandparents considered that "noise you kids listen to".

Enlightenment

What is normal about gender identity? As newer generations become more familiar and educated about alternative sexual orientations and gender identifications, the stigma of what those labels represent fades a bit and acceptance emerges. As we begin to form friendships with people with these labels, we realize that they are just that... people.

Our brains have an inherent need to categorize. With our five senses, we have a sensory overload of data that our brain processes and files away in different parts of our gray matter. In order to understand something new, the brain searches its memory for what that new thing most likely resembles. So, if the brain is familiar with drag queens and gay men, then the crossdressing man must fall under the same label based on similar attributes.

The pursuit of knowledge is unnecessary to most people because there typically is no reason to understand it beyond its generalities. It doesn't affect them in life so they remain oblivious to any other information on the subject. The problem arises when the person is confronted with the unknown and must make a quick determination based on the knowledge (or misinformation) they already possess.

Following In The Footsteps

In the last thirty to forty years, the homosexual community has made great strides for education and integration into society, gaining acceptance. But education is only as productive as the passion for the pursuit of that knowledge. As individuals took claim of their sexual identities and revealed themselves to those closest to them, the people they confided in now had an interest and responsibility to become educated defenders.

More recently, the transsexual community found itself in the spotlight with Chaz Bono (formerly Chastity) and Caitlyn Jenner (formerly Bruce). Countless other members of the community have also come forward. All were tortured with their true identities trapped in the wrong gender shell, finally deciding to make right what they considered wrong. Again, those closest to them tried to learn more. They asked questions and read literature. They chose to better understand their loved one's transsexual experience, finally willing and ready to hear their words.

As more people reveal their alternative sexual orientation or their true gender identity, more members of their family and friends become champions for them. It is easy to disown and to ostracize; it is difficult to expand one's understanding and acceptance of something foreign and new. It is even more challenging to defend loved ones against attack from others.

But it's an important pursuit.

Just like others in the rainbow spectrum of the LGBTQ community, the crossdresser is looking for acceptance. We don't want to continue to live in secret and under the glare of intolerance. Religious dogma plagues and vilifies us, ignorance mislabels us, and mischaracterization destroys the strength of our character.

We face the same challenges as those who have come before us, with one added wrinkle. I am not talking about my crow's feet or the laugh lines around my mouth, although those are pressing issues as well! While people have begun to wrap their minds around the concepts of sexual orientation and of transitioning individuals, they still furrow their brows with a puzzled expression as to why crossdressers do what they do.

Best Of Both Worlds

Understanding why a man loves a man or a woman loves a woman, or why a man wants to be a woman or a woman wants to be a man is becoming easier. The concept of why a man wants to dress as a woman for a few days a week or month is still difficult to contemplate. If the man isn't 1) gay, or 2) looking to transition to womanhood, then... why does he love to put on a bra and panties (if its not a fetish)?

Well, I don't have a really good answer for you. It could be a compulsion. I have heard that it must be an addiction. Perhaps because some crossdressers started doing it during puberty, they developed a sensory reward complex that made them want to do it again and again. There are emerging medical claims that theorize that the brain's chemistry and development play a part. There are many theories and studies that could be true or, at least, contributing factors.

Crossdressers flirt with the line between masculinity and femininity. We are chameleon in nature, able to change our outward appearance as the mood strikes. We walk a line in a pair of heels as well as we do in a pair of beat up Air Jordan Nike sneakers. For me, I can sport my Miami Vice Don Johnson scruff just as well as my Clinique liquid foundation and chubby black mascara. Conversely, I admit that I have more enjoyment when shopping for Savannah clothes, while my male side shopping is economical and disinterested in current fashion.

The beauty of being me – besides my physical awesomeness, haha – is that I can dance the night away with my gurlfriends on a Wednesday night as Savannah before returning to the workforce the next morning as drab ole me to clickity-clack on the keyboard for eight to ten hours. There is a measure of satisfaction in knowing I am not tied to one gender or the other.

For the gay and lesbian community, they discovered to whom they are attracted. The folks in the transitioning transgender community discovered who they were on the inside and decided to what degree they wanted to present themselves on the outside. Being of two genders does not make me better or worse than any other social group. It simply allows me freedom to be who I want to be without the need for permanence.

Balancing Acts

The cynic finds love with the idealist. The rebel with the conformist. The social butterfly with the bookworm. They help each other balance their lives

~ Joyce Brothers

Happiness is not a matter of intensity but of balance, order, rhythm and harmony.

~ Thomas Merton

Starting Lines

In order to *lead* a balanced life it is important to understand what the term means. It seems so easy a concept. But balance is like chess. It takes minutes to learn and years to master. Visualize a scale like you would see with the blind woman of justice - your balance scale of life – and visualize that it has several pans that hold the different components of your existence instead of just the two.

Now ask yourself a question. Do you have every element of your life in alignment and in perfect synchronicity? Are all the pans perfectly level with equal weight around the fulcrum? Or do you feel that you are being pulled or pushed too hard in any one direction? If you have a sense of being dragged down or that you haven't given enough weight to one of your pans of life, you may need to reassess your life's balance.

Keep in mind, though, that balance doesn't come in equal measure. Each component is not measured in units of time but in quality of its use. When you are in balance you experience a sense of calm, grounding and contentment. You feel more positive. Feelings of resentment don't creep into your head to nag you with an itch of dissatisfaction.

With crossdressing, there must be equilibrium. I bet the men reading this book are all smiles as they point out this sentence to their partner and say, *See? Savannah says I need equilibrium!*

Balancing The Scales

As with anything worth pursuing in life, equilibrium does not exist in a vacuum. Balance exists both internally and externally. Your sense of peace is for you alone, an internal balance that only you can master. Your surroundings, experiences and the people around you affect your external balance.

Internal balance is the calm that you master for the health of your body, mind and spirit.

- Balance the pursuit of knowledge against a quiet mind.
- Balance of giving and receiving love. It validates that we aren't isolated from the world. Outward love starts from within us. And we can only accept love if we allow it in.
- Balance of the physical body means eating well and proper exercise. It also involves treating yourself to… you guessed it… *treats*. To push the body too hard or to deny an indulgent experience is a surefire way to be unbalanced.

Internal balance is difficult enough, but there are all of the external elements to consider. What are those external things that are important to your fulfillment as a person?

- Having a good job and making money? Financial goals are great, but to push too hard in business without stopping a moment to take in the grander landscape of life is not balance.
- Having a family with two and a half kids, a dog, and a picket fence? Being responsible for your family and their health, but forgetting about being responsible for yourself is not balance.
- Cutting loose out on the town having a great time with friends? If that is all you are accomplishing, you will eventually burn out. And that (say it with me) is not balance

That all sounds too hard, Savannah! Just thinking about juggling of all those things is stressing me out!

And you would be right if we intended to look at a life-size balance all at once. Balance is fluid and ever changing. The things that make you feel a sense of calm change as you change. Each of the elements I mentioned above is positive, but taken to selfish extremes is not.

So when are we going to talk about my need to crossdress?

Yeah! When are we going to get my crossdressing partner to realize it isn't all about him?

Coming To An Accord

In the comments on the previous page lie the challenges for striking a balance between a crossdresser and his partner. So how do you do it? As we have discussed, everything needs to start on a level mental playing field. In the following pages, I am going to assume a scenario where the crossdresser has revealed himself to his partner. Where you go from here is up to you, but I hope I can give you a few tips to help make the transition easier.

First, crossdressers, be honest with yourself. Take a deep dive into the pool of understanding who you are and what makes you happy in life. If you're unsure of what you want, seeking therapy or an outside opinion may help to ground your thinking on the subject. If you cannot be honest with yourself and your partner, you already have a strike against you.

For you, dear partner, be honest with your crossdressing man. Share your thoughts and fears in as healthy a way as possible. I know that your heart is filled with trepidation and your head is filled with questions, but tackle one thing at a time in a way that is not demeaning or sharply edged toward him.

Next, start the examination process. You have both stated your sides, are processing intense emotions and fears, and have hundreds of questions to have answered. How can crossdressing become part of a balance between you? When will you experience the feelings of being pushed too far or pulled too far?

You will both feel mentally out of balance at this point. This is the uncomfortable stage where you both feel you are sacrificing too much for the other. The scales are weighing down on the other end of the fulcrum against you.

Don't despair.

Examine and intellectualize what you believe your balance to look like. Ask yourself, how will you achieve equilibrium for yourself and your partner that reflects that ideal? Both sides need to come to the table with what they believe to be appropriate.

Crossdressers, beware the Pink Fog. Do not mistake your partner's silence or agreement to mean that she is completely against or onboard with every idea and fantasy you have. You should not think that you now have the green light to race two hundred mile per hour into the feminine abyss.

Partners, you also cannot allow your inherent fears to wholly guide your decision-making. Rash judgments may unfairly curb what your crossdressing partner is allowed to do. Try to be a part of his development, not fight blindly against it.

You are trying to build a balance of understanding, acceptance and exploration that will be a positive experience for both of you.

So, how do we do that, Savannah?

Simple. Set goals and make plans. Set aside time to develop a familiarity (a routine) between you. Crossdressers, this is the time where you will probably start to dress for your partner as part of a full reveal for her. She may want to watch you transform or she may want to be waiting in the living room to see you fully dressed. Either way, this should be done in a controlled and safe environment, whether at home or on neutral ground. Take the experience slow.

Do not let emotional expectations rule the day. Take each step as small stepping-stones. Do not harbor fear. But if fear does rears its head, talk about it. Discuss it. Be honest, as it is always the best policy. You may find that you talk for a couple hours as a couple, forgetting that you both are dressed as women.

Shared Experiences

Your first experience is over.
What now, Savannah?
Reflect on what occurred.

- How did you handle the experience?
- Did you listen to what your partner had to say about it?
- How did you handle your own fears?
- How did you convey those feelings to your partner?
- How did you receive that criticism and respond to it?
- What are the thoughts for moving forward from here?

Remember, you have now shared an experience. Have gratitude for it. You may have been nervous, crossdresser. Your partner may have been filled with dread, fears and expectations. Reflect on the positivity of the event. You shared yourself with her. You, hopefully, spoke more in depth about tangential topics of crossdressing. Crossdresser, thank your partner for her part. Remember that this experience is not just about what you want. Don't forget that your partner is trying to recreate and modify what she considered was her balance in life; what she considered normal.

Be prepared.

Get together as a couple and set the ground rules for the immediate future. I know that sounds too rigid, not allowing for spontaneity and freedom of spirit. But, I assure you it is essential to set the groundwork for spontaneity.

What the heck are you talking about?

Well, for Jen and me, I told her that I wanted a relationship between us that rivaled what we had as man and woman, something with more intimacy. She was not prepared with that line of thinking. So we set ground rules. We were to be best girlfriends when out in public. If she felt comfortable with holding my hand or giving me a kiss or hug, she would initiate the affection. Although difficult to start thinking that way on my part, it allowed for both of us to know what was okay and what was just expectation that would preoccupy my head with what ifs.

Preparations set the stage for empowerment.

Each of you is still dealing with the shifting weights on the scales, trying to get the scale pans to settle. This will be an ongoing process as smaller weights are added and removed. Just like that doctor's office beam scale where the nurse slides the bigger weight rider across the beam notches then follows with the smaller weight on the second beam, the balance will come with incremental adjustments until the pointer settles on the centerline. Keep setting goals and ground rules. You will find that these efforts will allow you to do something groundbreaking in your partnership.

Always work together.

Work together to improve; to connect; to communicate. Share your feelings and concerns to each other in an open and loving way. You are together because you care for each other, and want the best for each other. Allow your partner to help challenge and vanquish your demons, as well as celebrate every success and have gratitude for every moment, too.

Keep it all in perspective.

Haters Hate

Let no man pull you so low as to hate him.
~ Dr. Martin Luther King, Jr.

Love is the master key that opens the gates of happiness, of hatred, of jealousy, and, most easily of all, the gate of fear.
~ Oliver Wendell Holmes, Sr.

Reading The Labels

Crossdressers belong to the larger umbrella of the LGTBQ community. The acronym currently stands for Lesbian, Gays, Transgender, Bisexual, and Questioning. The letters attempts to describe a diverse group of people with alternative sexual orientations and gender identities. Besides LGTB and Q are other letters that represent additional sub-groups that belong to the community.

A is for asexual. G can be used for gender queer instead of gay, and other designations such as gender creative or gender fluid. Q can also stand for queer. There is a letter for 'intersexual' and 'pansexual'. Every year the letters of the alphabet end up describing new groups.

It took years of education and understanding for me to decide to ride the coattails of the label of crossdresser. We used to be called transvestites, coined by Magnus Hirschfeld in 1910. It was always a more clinical term, especially since it comes from the

Latin *trans*, meaning "across" or "over", and *vestitus*, meaning "dressed" (Gross! Latin!). The term transvestite, or the slang tranny, was considered a dirty word when I grew up.

It wasn't until my mid-twenties that I recognized and spoke the word aloud for myself. It was a momentous day of acceptance for me and for my self-assignment to a larger community. Of course, I never really liked the word transvestite and eventually gravitated to the softer moniker of crossdresser. Even at that time, my acceptance of the label was still based on misunderstood and limited information.

It's Not Euphoric

There were dozens of other descriptive titles that I had never heard of or fully understood their meaning. Gender Dysphoria is the condition of feeling that one's emotional and psychological identity as a male or female is opposite of their biological assignment. Gender fluidity relates to a person who does not identify as having a fixed or permanent gender. Pansexuals do not limit themselves or their sexual choices based on their biology. There are dozens more, and new labels popping up all the time.

It is a daunting task to understand all of the labels out there and to find one that fits you. Many of us try on more than one title through our lives, hoping to find that *one* that describes us the best. There is an inherent flaw to this line of thinking, however.

All of these labels are wrought with their own shroud of limits and expectations. Some of the labels are exclusive of each other, with some defining a sexual preference and others defining a gender preference. How does one navigate through all of the available information to see what group one belongs?

A bigger problem as I see it is the labels themselves. Why do we need a label at all? Sure, we seek out classifications because our brains strive to have a basic foundation of who we are, but we don't have to live or limit ourselves to the tenets of those labels. We should understand that we have the ability to transcend the shackles of those labels – and become something more than the simple sum of our parts.

War Against The States (Of Being)

It's of the utmost importance that you strive to discover who you are, dear crossdresser. Once you have found a measure of peace, you are ready to include your partner in such matters as well. She is your confidant and, most times, more wise than you are willing to admit. Even if you are struggling to come to terms with who you wholly are, having a strong support system is crucial.

So, you have gotten that all out of the way. You now know who you are on the transgender spectrum. Congratulations! All seems right with the world. You are content. Your partner is coming along on this strange ride with you, to your utter amazement. So what else is there to worry about?

Every day is a reassessment of who you are and how your partner is coping. Every day is an affirmation that you are appropriately 1) selfish to your needs and, 2) selfless to the needs of your partner. It is you two against a world that fears us (taken straight out of context from any of a dozen Marvel X-Men comics).

The problem is that there is a big, uneducated, biased world out there. I know that some of us are lucky enough to have a circle of friends and family that supports and loves us unconditionally. There still is judgment and ridicule from many sides and from the oddest of sources.

We understand there will be resistance and resentment from those in our lives that don't have the knowledge or experience to accept us. Whom we confide in is based on the person's temperament, capacity for sympathy and empathy, and open mindedness. This is a dance we know the steps to, all too well. Although the closer the person is in our hearts, the more difficult it is to see the right next step to sharing, sometimes.

Most of us will never reveal our full self to our grandparents, parents, or siblings. It is just a burden that we do not wish to pass on to them, unnecessarily. Speaking for myself, I was proud to share my alternative feminine side to my sister. But I would be hard pressed to come up with a good reason to tell my parents.

Social Commentary

Friends, family and co-workers aside, there are other groups that we expect would rally behind us crossdressers. Focusing on social media – the place where all judgment and bullying is done at the end of a keystroke – I must shed light on a strange and hard truth. There are those in our own LGBTQ community that hold animosity against us.

I don't understand why, Savannah? I'm just a crossdresser!

Within the spectrum of alternative lifestyles, there are some that consider us *less than*. There are many reasons, I am sure. They may not comprehend why we do what we do. Remember when you thought that wearing women's clothes meant that you must be a homosexual or want to become a woman fulltime? There are some gays and transitioning individuals that also think that one of those two criteria must be at play.

A gay man may believe that we dress as women in order to attract men. Therefore, we must be using crossdressing as a cover to deny that we are also homosexual. Many transsexual men used crossdressing as their testing grounds to become comfortable with the idea that they should have been born a woman. Crossdressing for them was a gateway to their true gender nature. Therefore, we must also be in denial about our true gender identity.

Don't get me wrong. I have dozens of friends as discussed above, none of whom has ever treated me with any less respect and love than I showed them. Yet, there still persists a small but outspoken and angry voice of condemnation towards crossdressers.

These voices make their positions known through their social media postings. Their opinions seem to mostly be slanted toward the political and human rights arenas. These transsexual women spout venom against the lowly crossdressing males that have offended them. They point out that we are not serious about our gender identities.

How could that be? Aren't we all on the same side of things?

You would think so, but that assumption would be incorrect in these specific cases. Some transsexual women consider us hobbyists, semi-serious, or in denial about our true feminine identity. The reasons may stem from the fact that they understand what crossdressing meant to their own transition and are projecting those experiences onto us. I recognize that these women understand life based on how they have lived and what experiences led them to their own critical life decisions. But that is a very narrow point of view that does not allow for any other perspectives ... or for other reasons why people may enjoy crossdressing.

They condemn us out of fear and ignorance of who we are in comparison to them. Gay men and women continue to fight for their rights for civil union, equality in the workplace, and protection against discrimination. Transsexual women are also fighting for equal rights under the laws of the country, waist deep in the fight against discrimination and for proper health care (and other issues).

Their complaint is that we, the crossdressers, give them a bad name. Remember some of the crossdressing types that a man could be? Think of how those crossdressers are perceived in public. The general populace is not ready for a bearded man in a skirt (except the Scots and their kilts) or a businessman who enjoys wearing tights under his dress pants.

The perception ranges from embarrassment to avoidance by *regular* folk. Since transsexual MtF women strive to be normal women, they see our behaviors as stumbling blocks to their own social acceptance in everyday life and on Capital Hill. They consider us part time feminine enthusiasts at best, masquerading around in all our fetish and inappropriate glory for the night, before we slip back into our privileged male lives. All the while, these transsexual women are fighting for their right to live as women everyday.

What Makes A Woman?

I am all for equal rights for all groups that need special protections and accommodations due to ongoing ignorance and intolerance. The world is too big and diverse to want otherwise. We crossdressers are often frowned upon because we are able to slip back and forth across the lines between male and female. We enjoy both the privileges of being a man and the benefits of being a woman.

Does that make us less committed to our gender identities? I don't think so. Does that make us less of a woman? Maybe. Since we flirt between both identities, it does put crossdressers on a different layer of the spectrum than transsexual women.

I spend one to two hours at a clip to properly become Savannah and be proud of the persona I am presenting. I'm always concerned that I will fail to pass casual inspection by the masses, fearing scorn and disapproval from the public. Is the discipline to my feminine craft any less real and committed than the transsexual woman's pursuits of her own womanhood? I know that I don't think like a woman 24 hours a day, hence a critical distinction to the crossdresser's journey from that of a transsexual woman.

We are considered *less than* by some because we choose not to pursue a single permanence to our gender identity. We're able to lace up a corset and dance the night away, then strip down to our male suited business casual Polo and khakis for a day on the job. Is it fair to be thought that we are unsure of our identity just because we choose to embrace our gender duality?

The real question is, why is it a matter of fairness? Why can't we all subscribe to be the person we want to be? Should people be judged for their beliefs and decisions, especially when they are not disruptive or a negative influence to others around them? It is sad to realize that there is an abundance of backbiting within the LGBTQ community. Please remember that this is not a social commentary for all members of the community, only directed to those most vocal about their disdain for those they do not consider fit to bear the labels of transgender.

There are post-operative transsexuals that pass judgment on pre-operative transsexuals for not being serious enough about becoming women. Some members of both of the aforementioned groups pass judgment on non-transitioning crossdressers for not acknowledging their secret unknown desire to be women. And, of course, we non-fetish crossdressers pass judgment on some of the more *out there* crossdressing groups for giving us a bad name when they are in public.

You see how the crap all rolls downhill. There is a strange assumption that the transsexuals with SRS (sexual reassignment surgery) are the pinnacles of the male to female expression. Agreed that they are certainly the most extreme measure of attaining femininity, but we all demonstrate our femininity in the best way we understand how to do so.

Again, remember to find your balance. If you feel that mental push or pull that makes you uncomfortable or stressed, you are not in alignment with your authentic self. Interestingly, as some men transition into a more surgical expression of womanhood, you will find that they fade away from the crossdresser community events in general. They have become their *normal*. Therefore, they do not feel the need to continue associating with those they have transcended from. They have found their balance.

Just A Crossdresser

Let us go back to the earlier question.
I don't understand why, Savannah? I'm just a crossdresser!
Number one, you are not *just* anything. You are a person, first and foremost. The label of crossdresser does not devalue who you are in relation to someone else in the community hierarchy. In fact,

there is no hierarchy, only different groups of individuals striving to find their place in the world. Never allow other community labels to create chaos and discontent within your own heart. The knowledge of one's self is yours alone.

Second, be the best you that you can be. Be honest with yourself and with the others you have chosen to share your gender identity with. Always be reflective about where you are on your journey. Are you still on the road? Do you see your destination? Or have you already checked into the hotel of your gender identity and are sipping Mai Tais by the pool?

Lastly, have respect. Have respect for yourself and for others around you. This obviously includes those closest to you in your life, but also should include those who come in contact with you in either form you choose to present. We are our own worst enemies when it comes to acceptance on the larger stage of life. Hold your head high, have confidence, be understanding, and be kind (and remember to rewind!).

My Better Half

Everything has its beauty but not everyone sees it.
~ Confucius

Friends show their love in times of trouble, not in happiness.
~ Euripides

Show And Tell

Hopefully, the preceding stories of crossdressers and their partners trying to survive or thrive gives you some insight that you can do the same for yourselves. I won't try to convince you that every relationship works. I can't tell you that everything will just fall into place and you will live happily ever after. But I can tell you that an open heart, an honest and full dialogue, and a will to find the deeper meaning within each other and us will provide you the strongest foundation and best chance to succeed.

And why shouldn't we succeed? The best things we have going for us is our love for each other – whatever form we take – and having a deeper understanding of our partners. For us crossdressers, we try to become the best version of ourselves. I don't mean to say that we are only the best version of ourselves when dressed as women. If that were how we were thinking, we should probably be on the path to full womanhood. Instead, I am only trying to illustrate that by understanding our duality we allow ourselves to empathize with others in a way that some men never will.

The trouble with crossdressers (gasp, I am actually admitting this?!) is that we sometimes lose sight and perspective of others when we dress. Many times it is all about us. If we still dress in secret, those scarce moments are a euphoric series of obsessive minutes or hours that are strung together to get our *fix*, like an addict.

Because we tend to feel that we are still considered undesirables and misunderstood by most groups, we have a sense that we must fulfill our feminine needs behind closed doors. The urge to hide our authentic selves from those closest to us is a slippery slope of secrecy that will eventually gnaw away at our happiness and bond with our loved ones.

This doesn't mean that we should go out and tell the world who we are. There are many crossdressers that apply a 'Need to Know' philosophy to who they tell. Do your aging parents need to know you dress as a woman from time to time? Is there a value to telling? You may have shared your secret with them, but now they have to cope with that knowledge and wrestle with sharing or keeping that secret too. They could commiserate with each other, if told, but why tell? You need to weigh the reasons why sharing is important.

In the revealing department, I usually follow my heart. I reveal myself to my partner on the day that I know there is long-term potential for the relationship. I usually say it's because I'm too lazy to lie about who I am, but I feel that full disclosure is more important than a relationship built on what I feel would be a shoddy foundation. For friends and family, I usually get a Savannah-sense (trademark pending!) in my heart that says, 'You should share Savannah with this person'. I then think on it for a bit before deciding to either expand my Savannah family or continue to keep *her* to myself.

The Same, But Different

This chapter is not about sharing with others.
Sorry about the tangential thinking.
Actually... wait... this chapter is about sharing. It is about sharing the best parts of us with others. The name of the chapter is entitled Our Better Half, for goodness sake. We want to share our better half with our better half. There is nothing I wouldn't give for a full relationship with Jen, both of us in love with every facet of the other. I am a hopeless optimist and romantic that way.

I think it is important to strive to be the Better Half. In that, I mean we should exude our best qualities regardless of our attire. Why should the clothing diminish the caliber of the moral character we present to the world? Clothing is an expression of us; it does not dictate a cookie cutter stereotype. Empathy and kindness do not require the presence of a garter belt to be conveyed (although it sometimes helps!).

As a man I am sensitive. I defer to others and listen to what they have to say. I am quiet and reserved, willing to speak up when I feel I have enough information to give a quality and intelligent response. I am empathetic. I am an introvert in some new social situations, but can be very outgoing when I am comfortable with my surroundings.

As Savannah, I am sensitive. I defer to others and list–
Wait!

Living with Crossdressing: Defining a New Normal

Are you telling me you were going to spit out the same attributes as Savannah as you did for your male side?

Of course! I am essentially the same person, regardless of what I am wearing. The clothing only allows me to be the fuller version of me.

Wait. What?

I know it's confusing. Believe me, it's confusing for us crossdressers, too. Most of us will never be able to sit down with our partner and adeptly answer that one pressing question, "Why do you do it?" We dress because it feels right.

Feels good, you mean.

Yes, dressing does feel good.

But it also feels right.

It seems normal to us. There is something that drives us. Call it addiction, compulsion, or any of a number of other terms to describe the desire to dress. But at the end of the day, it is still just us as us. To deny who we are could be catastrophic to our sense of wellbeing and our sense of happiness.

If dressing provides us comfort and a measure of calm and confidence, then it may help to illustrate the idea that a male crossdressers' femininity is an extension of his whole self. I do not have multiple personalities, but I do have more freedom to express myself as Savannah. I touch more (although Jen can attest that I am pretty touchy-feely no matter what) when around both men and women, am more confident to dance and let myself loose a bit, and may listen to what people have to say more than I usually do (which I feel is a lot, even in male mode).

Crossdressing allows for an escape from the stresses of everyday life. The act of dressing is ritualistic in nature, filled with movements that can serve to center us. If I'm not rushed to get ready for an outing, I find the act of *becoming* Savannah just as therapeutic as *being* Savannah. The motions of applying foundation and eye shadow are calming. The donning of a wig and bodycon dress is like armor against the hordes of stresses and fears laying siege at the gates of the kingdom.

Where we find solace in lace, satin and silk, real women may find the same comfort in an old oversized sweatshirt from college or a favorite pair of yoga pants or, maybe, a pair of fuzzy bunny slippers. We are drawn to what we are drawn to – no matter our gender. And speaking of gender, I'm not forgetting the most important Better Half. I have just decided to save the best for last.

The Best Half

This is where I would usually start gushing about Jen. She would start rolling her eyes at my mushiness and accolades; only partially believing what I say about her is true. Much of the time she simply doesn't believe those things in herself.

In some of my reading for enlightenment, I have come across the notion that we are so bristled at our own identity and in the belief of who we think we are that we cannot pull ourselves out of our own perspective.

Have you ever received a compliment? Has someone said something nice about your clothes or hair? I'm sure that you have. Have you found yourself saying, "What? This old thing?" or "Thanks, but it cost me a fortune for this haircut!"? What you're doing is deflecting the compliment because you do not believe in its sincerity. Not because you think the person who complimented you is being unkind or sarcastic, but because you don't believe in the truth of the words as they relates to you.

Keep that in mind the next time someone says something nice about you. In a cynical world, I'm sure there could be an endgame for every compliment. But in my world, I choose to accept the compliment with a "Thank you", even if I may not believe the kind words being spoken.

Eventually, you will believe.

In the meanwhile, I will continue to shower my girlfriend with the acclaim and compliments she rightly deserves. She has sacrificed much when she agreed to continue our relationship. She could have had a *normal* relationship with a nice guy without the baggage of a make-up case and an additional closet full of feminine clothes.

That is my belief.

But is it a truth?

Maybe she loves me because she sees that I am someone more evolved than the *normal* guy. I mean, my girlfriend never has to worry about being a football season widow (not to say that crossdressers can't be sports fanatics), she doesn't have to worry about washing dishes after spending an hour cooking, getting something girlie for the bedroom, or me getting into a macho bullshit pissing contest with another dude, etc.

She loves me because of who I am, even if she is still coming to terms with the feminine presentation. Savannah is a façade that hides the masculinity that she is attracted to but, after some time with me as *her*, those walls are slowly starting to come down.

There is a good reason that Jen is my better half. After our first romantic encounter's infamous words, "Hey, I have something to show you", Jen read all she could on the subject and sought out SOCD (significant others of crossdressers) websites and forums in an effort to find support and information. She was smart to NOT jump in headlong after the reveal.

What do you mean, 'smart'?

When some CD partners jump in with both feet in an attempt to support their men, they may find that they are overwhelmed with the onslaught of new information and revelations. When jumping in so quickly (and blindly, maybe), the partners are setting up a bar of expectation for their crossdressers. Suddenly, all of the men's hopes and fantasies are coming true. He is so happy that she is happy right along side him. That is, until there comes an episode, question, or situation that halts her in her tracks.

Imagine you are in a dragster (maybe a little pun intended) waiting for the starting tree of lights to blink from red to yellow to green. You find out about your partner's crossdressing (light turns green) and hit the accelerator. Wheels spin, smoke billows out and you defy the laws of proper speed limits as you race down the track (outings, events, romantic encounters with your CD). Then, he brings up some stray comment about a fear of transitioning. Your dragster has just hit the side barricades at over two hundred miles per hour. You will survive the experience of the crash, but that moment of impact is going to hurt.

Jen took the opposite approach. Since she had never been in a dragster, she harnessed in, tried to familiarize herself with the cockpit instruments (still funny!), and started taking test runs down the track. She backed up the dragster to the starting line after each run until she felt comfortable for a real head-to-head race.

That analogy was exhausting… and exhilarating!

Truth be told, I was afraid that the slow pace was an admission that Jen would never warm up to the idea of being in a relationship with a crossdresser. We have spent a couple years gaining momentum... and we are not even close to hitting top speed (or red-lining, thank goodness). She was smart in her approach, in terms of how she needed to deal with this new knowledge. A new normal does not just happen overnight.

The New Normal

Jen is definitely dealing with the notion that she and I can be the new normal. And that paradigm shift is not something that happens instantly. For some, like with Melissa and Annabelle, there was no shift in thinking because Annabelle was already attuned to alternative lifestyle living. For others, for the vast majority of women, there has already been established a way of thinking – men wear male clothes, women wear female clothes.

Fascinating, really. What the heck is a paradigm shift again?

A paradigm shift (pronounced "pair a dime") is defined as a fundamental change in approach or underlying assumptions. It is when behavior is permanently altered based on a new dynamic. A perfect modern example of a paradigm shift is the invention of the smartphone. Look at any teenager or urban professional and you will find them staring at their iPhone or Android checking emails, taking selfies, getting directions, and playing Candy Crush. Fast becoming extinct is the need for Rand McNally maps when traveling, needing to be at our desks to be connected to the office, or saving shoeboxes full of memories.

Redefining the way to view how people are *supposed* to dress is a difficult concept to shake off. Early in Jen's life (as a reminder), she came home from work to find her partner sitting on the couch with a shaved body and attired in lingerie and garters. It was a shock and off-putting. She went away and put it out of her mind. It was wrong for him to be wearing women's clothes. That was not how the world worked. Men were masculine and women were feminine.

How do you break that social construct? How do you break the idea that men must be masculine? I mean, women can have masculine traits. Tomboy girls are accepted. Jen told me that she was brought up to believe that men were the superior gender, ruling the world. She made the comment that it didn't matter if women were superior to men in every way, because, in the end, the dominating intelligence and cunning of a woman would never trump the closed fists of a man.

In that example, the only reason that men are superior is because they can beat each other up. Isn't that how wars are waged? And doesn't that mean that women would have to compete with men on their masculine level in order to feel that they are worthy of trust and equality of any kind? So, here we crossdressers sit with our partners wondering how to accept a man that would give up all of his male superiority in order to affect a feminine persona.

Setting The Ground Rules

Like Debra and Eden, Jen set some dress code ground rules early. She didn't want me to wear overly frilly or lacy panties, or anything too feminine in color. She didn't want me to wear lingerie or nightgowns to bed.

I was crushed that I was forced to be stifled from the freedom to wear what I wanted. But I abided the rules for the sake of the relationship and for the simple fact that she allowed us to continue in the first place (remember, we crossdressers don't feel worthy a lot of the time, anyway, so we grasp at the hope that we and our partners will succeed). The rules, once in place, weren't terrible concessions to make. I didn't try to overdo my dressing in front of her. That allowed Jen to slowly reshape what she thought of a man in female clothes.

She would see me wearing simple cut women's underwear. She became desensitized to it. But not desensitized in a bad way. She described it as making the visual and cognitive connection "no big deal, anymore". Jen even said to me that she found it an "interesting phenomenon how while it still feels weird to see you in panties, the thought of seeing you in boxers or tightie whities seems even more weird".

That is an important component to this re-education process (that sounds ominous, Clockwork Orange fans, doesn't it?). Instead of negative reinforcement, Jen was able to become accustomed to my *low-grade* dressing because nothing bad happened. I didn't surprise her fully dressed as Savannah, demanding kinky sex (like her previous experience). My dressing might have been the beat of a butterfly's wings in China, but no tsunami blew through the California coast as a result.

So that level of dressing became the new normal.

There wasn't much discussion about what was an appropriate next step. I asked how I would know when she was comfortable with my dressing. She shrugged and told me that we would both know when it happened. I would push the boundaries a little bit from time to time, testing the acceptance waters. When it became too much – when my three steps forward became her two steps back – we readjusted to what was tolerable.

Never wear tights on the couch to watch television for three evenings in a row, gurlfriends. Just giving you a heads-up! That's

Living with Crossdressing: Defining a New Normal

what happened. She spoke up that she wasn't feeling comfortable with my choice to dress. The first day she was ok with it. The second day she was troubled, but didn't say anything because she didn't feel it was her right to demand what I should be able to wear in our own home. By the third day, her reservations about keeping quiet were overwhelmed by her own need to "be ok".

It's a compromise, as is anything worthwhile. Compromise, with understanding, is one of the cornerstones for anyone in a relationship. Remember the ideas for balance in one's life. All of those lessons are compounded when you need to take into account the feelings and needs of another person.

Jen and I still test the boundaries of normalcy. We go to transgender-friendly restaurants for GNO (Girls' Night Out) with other crossdressers and their partners. The other patrons at the restaurant pay us no mind. The restaurant staff loves us and treats us wonderfully. Nothing bad happens. Positive reinforcement happens.

Presto! A new normal happens.

Jen can look back two or three years and see that she's not the same person that she was. Her views on the world, on the crossdressing community, and on me have fundamentally changed. Maybe in another year Jen will be sitting in Outback Steakhouse with Savannah and reminisce about that silly phase of our relationship where she was worried that people would be offended, judgmental, or angry at the sight of us.

Oh, silly us!

There is nothing to say that something bad can't happen. There can always be a stray outspoken or drunk individual whose ignorance drives his or her bigotry and venom toward our kind. Jen could experience that negative reaction and stumble a step or two, but she can still be confident that she has set the forms and poured the concrete under her for curing foundation. For her, it is important to have a solid base so that when bad things happen, she can be confident in her own convictions to take on all comers.

Patience is a virtue – perhaps the greatest virtue.

For you, dear crossdresser, it is important to have patience, understanding and recognition for what your partner is going through as she walks on the path of this journey with you. She is coping with her own tolerance and acceptance as she strives to become accustomed to what she considers her new normal. Crossdressers, if you are reading this... don't screw it up!

Last Words On The Subject

The idea that crossdressing is normal is a notion that may never materialize. Members of the gay and lesbian community enjoy a measure of acceptance. Transitioning men and women are starting to be recognized with a growing understanding, if not total acceptance. Both groups are considered by most to be 'born that way'.

Non-transitioning crossdressers are looked at as having a choice. We keep a foot in both the masculine and feminine worlds. With no proof that crossdressers are wired differently from normal folk, we are considered just a bunch of weirdos who like to get off by wearing frocks and panties. Would society see us in a better light if it were clinically proven that we were psychologically and mentally wired different from other men? Would we be more accepted? Or would the general public see us as creatures worthy of their pity? Maybe, they would try to cure us like religion and medicine tried to do in the past for homosexual men and women?

It is still too early to tell. We will have to keep each other informed. Stay tuned.

Sex, Lies & Videotape

Unexpressed emotion will never die. They are buried alive and will come forth later in uglier ways.

~ Sigmund Freud

No man has the right to dictate what other men should perceive, create or produce, but all should be encouraged to reveal themselves, their perceptions and emotions, and to build confidence in the creative spirit.

~ Ansel Adams

Dear Diary

Hey, Savannah?

Yes, dear reader?

Why are crossdressers so into themselves?

Why do you ask?

Because Facebook is rampant with trashy pics of crossdressers in bars acting slutty.

What makes you think they are acting?

Ba-dum-bum! Hey-ooh!

Sorry, that was silly and a forced dialogue for a cheesy punch line. Wait... did I just say 'cheesy'? That sounds like a segue to me.

Many crossdressers love to snap pictures of themselves and their friends while out. They love to post to their Instagram,

SnapChat and Facebook pages (and to whatever social media will be in vogue after the printing of this book!). Is the practice different than cis-men and women doing the same thing on their own social media outlets?

Taking photos is simply a form of chronicling one's life in a social diary format. It quickly shows us where we have been, the people we were with, and a reminder of the experiences we have had. I, personally, do not take many pictures of myself while out. I have wonderful friends that do that for me. Before I transform back into a pumpkin, I end up taking a few pics at the end of the night to immortalize my night out and to see how well my makeup held up through the evening's affairs.

Taking pictures of our feminine selves also serves to validate that we can actually pass as women. Looking back on a night to see our wide smiles serves as a reminder that we are tangible and *complete*. No one can take that away from us. Of course, we are just like teenage girls when we take pics. We sift and swipe through the gallery until we find the one or two photos that we are not horrified by to post (deleting the rest).

But why are there so many slutty pics?

Scandalous

Well... ahem... some crossdressers are... how can I put this... working girls. There are some transsexuals and crossdressers who are in the risqué trade. They post videos and photos in public social media galleries to gain a following. Then, once they reach a critical mass of followers, they direct them to other sites to see more risqué pics and videos so that they can make money. Some make money with paid subscribers and some make money through advertising clicks.

Much of what you may have come across is just a part of the larger sex industry. It is no different than any other segment – girl-on-girl, boy-on-girl, etc. – that draws in people who like that sort of thing. Pornography is a ten billion dollar (with a B) industry, and there is a market for all types of fetishes. Yes, when you venture into those types of salacious images and videos, you are now venturing into the fetish arena. I could say that these gurls and girls are just trying to find a way to make money (and I have heard that from one gurl who had started up her second pay-for-pic website), but they do serve a demographic that can reinforce what people tend to think all crossdressers are.

Let's think about that for a moment. Women have been portrayed as whores, sluts and nymphomaniacs in porn for years, and yet women walk around freely without being branded as such. Many men would like to think real women are like the ones in those videos but, in general, that line of thinking is wish fulfillment as opposed to stereotyping women in the real world.

Crossdressers face the same things, but in reverse. Since we are misunderstood, people feel validated when they see online *proof* that supports their general hypothesis. We see what we want to see, and discard all the proof that fails to support our assertions, regardless of how compelling that proof may be. Be sure to look at any Internet photo or video with an open mind, comparing them to how *the industry* presents other groups' seedy and scandalous sides. Typically, the more professional the image, the more professional the gurl (unless there is a portrait studio reference!)

Compensation

Of course, not all posted pics are from the porn industry. We are all guilty of posing for those pics where we are bumping out our hips, thrusting out our chests, and running our hands through our hair, trying to look as sexy as we possibly can.

Yeah. Slutty!

The simplest explanation is usually the best. In an effort to strike as feminine a pose as possible, we over-compensate. We mimic what we understand femininity to be. And because we are trying so hard to undo our masculine attributes, we go big with the flair in order to fool the camera into believing that first, we are not ten pounds heavier than we are and, second, that we are not burly men failing at our female presentation.

The camera never lies, although we wish it would. It is a cruel mistress that always reflects back on us what we truly are – for good or ill.

Adept crossdressers understand how to minimize their frame and actions, using their bodies to mislead their masculine appearance. Some crossdressing men are slender of frame and pass easily, but others (like me) have to cheat. We add padding to our hips to re-proportion our frames in alignment with our broader shoulders and add a corset or waist cincher to affect a more hourglass shape. We draw the elbows in to minimize our silhouette. We are looser with our fingers and wrists to extend our feminine flow.

It is always a tireless and tiring practice to pursue our optimal femininity. We continually remind ourselves of our progress through our photo chronology. And since most of us still see our male faces under the makeup, we are really never content with our results. We gush to other crossdressers about how pretty their dresses are, how great the shape and flow of their new wigs are, and how we love the shade of their new lipstick, but we can never see in ourselves what we automatically see in them. Maybe we have blinders to our own beauty because we validate only external sources of it.

Yes, we are just as guilty of that derailing line of thinking as everyone else. Maybe, that makes us just as human.

Probing Questions

Can a mortal ask questions which God finds unanswerable? Quite easily, I should think. All nonsense questions are unanswerable.

~ C.S. Lewis

Questions are never indiscreet, answers sometimes are.

~ Oscar Wilde

Ask Me Anything!

As we start winding down this book, dear reader, I decided to have our contributing couples raise some questions that need to be answered by either the crossdresser or his partner. These are questions that should be thought through and considered.

There is no single truth or wrong answer.

Speak honestly and listen with intent.

Remember that as the respondent, sometimes, you need to take a moment to shovel deeper than you want to in order to dig out the truth.

Jen and I asked the couples we interviewed what questions they had on their minds now that the wife or girlfriend knew that her husband or boyfriend was a crossdresser. These are the raw responses as we received them, without filters or restraint. Some are thoughtful musings while others are based on frayed emotions and fear. We do not intend to answer these questions, as every individual will have a different response based on where they are in their journey.

The Questions

1. *FOR HIM:* What is so confining about your male persona that you think dressing as a woman could change or alleviate?
2. *FOR HIM:* What word or words describe how you feel living as a man?
3. *FOR HIM:* Does dressing in private make you feel vulnerable or empowered?
4. *FOR HIM:* When you move on from a private setting to a public setting dressed as a woman, how does that change how you feel?
5. *FOR HIM:* What have you gained from coming out?
6. *FOR HIM:* What have you jeopardized by coming out?
7. *FOR HIM:* Why the secrecy with your partner when all these years she confided in you about her own mistakes and issues?
8. *FOR HIM:* Why not confide in your partner? You said you considered her your best friend.
9. *FOR HIM:* Why didn't you tell your partner the truth when she was young, liberal and carefree; as opposed to when she is worn out from life, disappointed, and afraid to make it on her own.

Living with Crossdressing: Defining a New Normal

10. *FOR HIM:* Why do you think some male-to-female crossdressers are more attracted to and excited by other crossdressing men than they are to cis-women?
11. *FOR HIM:* Why do I have to continue to be the one to initiate conversation about your crossdressing?
12. *FOR HIM:* Why do I have to coax you to crossdress after you plead with me that you have a need to dress?
13. *FOR HIM AND HER:* What percentage of crossdressers do you think go on to transition?
14. *FOR HIM:* Why does a crossdresser's urge to dress wane from time to time? Is there a hormonal cause?
15. *FOR HIM:* What percentage of crossdressers do you think are still *in the closet*?
16. *FOR HIM:* Do men who identify themselves as strictly crossdressers feel they suffer from Gender Identity Dysphoria?
17. *FOR HIM:* Why do you take more pictures of yourself when you are dressed as a woman?
18. *FOR HIM:* Why can't you understand that I am willing to participate and be involved with your crossdressing?
19. *FOR HIM AND HER:* Should we involve other members of our family? Which friends should we tell and who needs to know?
20. *FOR HIM:* Do you dress for sexual release?
21. *FOR HIM:* Do you find that you feel more sensual or sexual when you are dressed?
22. *FOR HER:* Will you ever fully accept me as a partner with dual identities?
23. *FOR HER:* Could you ever become a defender of my crossdresser?

You Can't Handle The Truth

Truth is everybody is going to hurt you; you just gotta find the ones worth suffering for.

~ Bob Marley

Three things cannot be long hidden: the sun, the moon, and the truth.

~ Buddha

Call Back

Remember earlier in the book where we talked about the toddler and the blanket that would calm him? Dear partner, does any of that now ring with more truth, or at least more feasibility, as it may relate to your crossdresser? In life, truth is what you make it.

And that is all I want from my crossdresser, Savannah. All I want is the truth.

And you deserve no less, dear partner.

Each person in a relationship should be treated as an equal. Truths need to be told, for they are the easiest to say. Yet, somehow speaking the truth is one of the most difficult things to do, especially after secrets have been locked away for a long time.

The bricks and poured concrete laying the foundation of the secret bunker are filled with misdirection, half-truths and omissions. Armed sentries of fear and shame stand post at every conceivable entrance and exit into that bunker. All the while, the keeper of the secret sits a mile underground in a ten-foot square gray-washed room sitting atop a chained and locked crate that hums like a bomb ready to detonate. It is an existence where the heart races, sweat pours down the brow, and the walls constantly pulse and close in to suffocate the last vapors of oxygen out of the lungs.

But the alternative, to release the secret into the world, seems like it would be akin to opening Pandora's box and setting loose its contained evils to the world. Better to stand guard as a martyr than to trust and believe in the good in our fellow man and woman. According to the Greek myth, when Pandora opened the lid and released the evils upon the world she closed it in time to keep one of the contents from escaping, Elpis – translated as hope (or expectation).

The secret of crossdressing, to many, is like releasing the evils upon the world, its wraithlike talons poised to destroy all in its mindless path. The crossdresser needs to understand when it comes to his partner, there is always hope. Knowing our partner and ourselves allows hope to guide the truth from the box to the light.

One thing was left in Pandora's Box after she was able to close its lid. What we still hold in our hearts against the evils of the world is that same thing – hope.

What Is Truth?

Are you familiar with the parable of the six blind men who were set to describe a pachyderm standing in front of them? One described its rough and round legs as tree trunks. Another ran his hands along pointed ivory and thought it to be a spear. A third grabbed at a tail and considered it a rope. Yet another found the animal's trunk and recoiled with the assertion that he had come across a snake.

Each knew the truth, as he understood it. Their experience shaped how they could describe and reference something new to them. The same could be said about the partners of crossdressers. Many understand crossdressing in a very vague sense, quickly formulating an opinion after being told about their partner's proclivities. Their minds piece together what they know of gay men, celebrity cases of men transitioning into women and vice versa, and strange uncles who thought it would be a hoot to dress up in drag for Halloween.

A crossdressing partner's understanding is shaped by their exposure (or lack there of) to the alternative gender community. So, of course, questions will be asked that may sound harsh to us crossdressers. Are you gay? Do you want to be a woman? We may instantly take offense at such questions. How could they dare ask such things? Please understand that these questions are not asked out of spite, but in a pursuit of knowledge about a part of your life that was sheltered from them.

Partners have a right to ask any question. And you, dear crossdresser, have a responsibility to tell them the truth to the fullest extent of your own understanding. At that moment in time, if you don't know the answer, what do you do? Don't circle C like was suggested for when you took a multiple-choice pop quiz. Tell your partner, "I don't know", or whatever the truth is. Then explore for the answers.

Those blind men were really silly, weren't they? A snake and a tree trunk... what idiots, right? Nope! They qualified based on what they understood. It is our job, dear crossdressers, to help illuminate what it truly means to be who we are.

But I can't explain who I am, Savannah! I don't even understand why I do what I do.

Why not? You have been doing this crossdressing thing for either a little while or for a lifetime. Have you never reflected on the whys? Not the whys of the roots of attraction. That is a deeper question, like why does a gay man like men. There may be one answer or there may be a hundred answers... or there may be no answer to that question. But to analyze what we like about it, what comfort we find in it, and what pleasures we derive from it are all attainable answers if we decide to look for them. Living a life without understanding is a life without enlightenment.

Truth is also enlightenment and wisdom. The truth is only as true as our understanding. If asking the question, "Why do you go to church?" results in the answer, "Because my momma always took me...", then are we being honest with the reasons why we hold our religion so tightly? Our perception of truth is only as good as what we *can* see and what we *choose* to see.

Those blind men, had they brought their collected wisdom together, could have discovered a new truth and posed the answer of an elephant to those who were asking them to decipher the animal before them. That is also true with the truth. We may understand our own crossdressing and our partners may have their own notions of enlightenment on the subject of transgenderism, but have we looked outside ourselves to learn more about the community at large? Have we as crossdressers done any reading? Have we gotten together to share our experiences with others like us? Have we taken in that information and reflected on how that knowledge fits into our own lives?

Pursuit Of Truth

Continuing to use those blind men as our example, I asked whether they would have realized that the animal before them was an elephant had they brought their collected wisdom together in collaboration. But if they did, would that be the truth? Is the elephant really an elephant?
Of course it is, Savannah? What else would it be?
Well, true, it's an elephant because a bunch of zoologists way back in the day (Dane Cook says it was a Wednesday) decided that they knew best how to classify the animal. So that assumption takes us back to understanding how the world works through labels. We understand the world based on our knowledge and experience. Do we know all we need to know about men who crossdress? Have all crossdressing men willingly come forward to participate in an international census that would take all of our answers and crunch the numbers into a statistically significant and sound profile of who we are and why we do what we do?

Of course that output would only be accurate if the right questions were asked to begin with. Can someone (or a group of someones) ask the right questions to a crossdresser if they themselves have never had the urge to crossdress?
So have the crossdressers compose the questions.
That wouldn't work either, because most crossdressers only understand themselves (and even that understanding is not always complete).
So now what? I feel like we are going in circles.
We are going in circles, dear reader.
That is the point.
Are you confused? Are you wondering where to go from here?

Yes.

Good.

Learning begins with the act of asking questions. You have to be willing to truly hear the answers and process them into an understanding that is ever expanding. Answers should lead to more questions. There are no dead ends, only opportunities to fill in the gaps. We can't deny information because it runs contrary to our current beliefs.

Keep an open mind.

Ask pressing questions of your partner and really listen to the answers given.

Hold your partner to nothing less than the truth.

Reflect on why you hold to your beliefs.

Is an elephant only a truth if it is comprised of a sum of its parts? Is the animal only truth because it is the most commonly held and accepted belief as to what it is? Or are we constantly discovering new things about life that change the way we see things?

In the 4th century BCE, the Greeks believed with certainty that Earth was the center of the known universe. In the 16th century, Copernicus theorized that the sun was the center of the universe and that the Earth orbited around it. In the last century, entirely new galaxies have been discovered, increasing our understanding of an *expanding* universe and our place within it.

The Earth is held up on the shell of a giant turtle.

Not true.

The Earth is flat and sailing ships can fall off the edges into the abyss.

Didn't happen.

The moon is made of cheese.

A fairy tale.

Homosexuals are an evil abomination and need to be cured.

Religious dogma.

Crossdressers are all gay, dress as a fetish, and secretly want to be biological women.

Not all of us.

Reluctance

The bed is a bundle of paradoxes: we go to it with reluctance, yet we quit it with regret; we make up our minds every night to leave it early, but we wake up our bodies every morning to keep it late.

~ Ogden Nash

When I have reached a summit, I leave it with great reluctance, unless it is to reach for another, higher one.

~ Gustav Mahler

Accurate Quotes

I hope you have enjoyed reading the quotes that have accompanied the chapters. I selected each of them in the hopes that they would resonate with the topics being discussed. I also chose them because, regardless of when they were written or spoken, they are poignant and relevant... and I tried my best to treat them with reverence.

These two quotes are especially heartfelt on a personal level as it comes to my experiences as Savannah. While difficult to understand our motivations as to why we dress in the first place, we do enjoy the act of dressing. I do not look too far or too deeply to uncover the reasons why I think the way I do. As long as I am not hurting others close to me or myself, the root causes seem less important than understanding and embracing me as a full person.

Changing between forms can be a difficult transition. That's the simplest statement I can make on it. The art of becoming my feminine self is a sometimes frustrating, often-painstaking endeavor, taking far too much time and effort to achieve a semblance of womanliness that I am satisfied with. Why can't it just be a snap of the fingers to get the vision of what's in my head onto my physical form? I know I said that the act of applying makeup and getting into all our feminine attire is a calming process – it is – but that process also serves as a reminder that we are not the women that we want to present as.

Sometimes we can't even be bothered to get up the motivation to dress. Some crossdressers I have talked to are happy to dress once every couple of months. It is not an incessant need for all of us all of the time. It doesn't consume every waking moment. It is something we like to do on occasion when the mood strikes us. In her interview, Debra stated that he wanted a loving relationship with his wife, with the ability to dress as Debra *when the mood struck*.

Conversely, for me, the act of unbecoming is also sometimes difficult. While most women can't wait to kick off their heels, rip off those pantyhose and get a hand unzipping and slipping off that dress, most crossdressers want their feminine experience to last as long as it can before having to return to everyday life. When I get home, I like to take those selfies that I didn't take while out experiencing life as Savannah. I like to take a physical inventory of how I look, reflect for a moment on Savannah as a human being, assess what I could do better for next time, and say my silent goodbyes.

Is This Goodbye?

Could we see when and where we are to meet again, we would be more tender when we bid our friends goodbye.

~ Ouida

Spread love everywhere you go. Let no one ever come to you without leaving happier.

~ Mother Teresa

Parting Is Such Sweet Sorrow

William Shakespeare may have said it best. Juliet uttered those words to her lover Romeo. She acknowledged the feelings that accompanied their reluctance to part ways for the evening, but also affirmed their longing for the next moments where they could share their hearts' love for each other in person.

Crossdressing is like that for some of us. We pour our hearts into our craft of feminine being, living those moments like they are our last, then suffer our sweet sorrow for the end of each feminine episode and our longing for the next time where we can feel so free and whole as a person again.

I pursue my love of the written word, provide positivity and hope for people around me, and devote my whole heart to my true love. I do these things as both a man and as Savannah (except writing, since it is somewhat difficult to type with French-manicured nails).

Living with Crossdressing: Defining a New Normal

I long for a world where our masculinity and femininity are both celebrated as normal. I long for a world that doesn't judge us on currently established social constructs of what makes a man a man and a woman a woman. Maybe intolerance will become tolerance, and tolerance will become acceptance, as people learn more about what a crossdresser is and is not. Understanding of what our individual truth is may become an enlightenment of a new universal truth.

I hope I have helped you, dear reader. I may not have answered all or even a few of your questions. I hope, at the very least, I helped you to ask more questions of yourself and of your partner. The pursuit of knowledge comes at a price. That price should be gladly paid in order to come out the other side a stronger and more enlightened individual.

Don't be afraid of your truth.

Cast aside your assumptions.

Show honor to yourself and to your partner.

Just take that first step and show up.

With warmest regards and love,
Savannah Hauk

Resources & Bibiographies

Deloto, Barbara, Thomas Newgen. *An Addicted Cross-Dresser, Married and a Happy Ending – A True Story.*
CreateSpace Independent Publishing Platform, 2013.

Boyd, Helen. *My Husband Betty: Love, Sex, and Life with a Crossdresser.*
PM Publishers Inc, 2003.

Rudd, Peggy J. *My Husband Wears My Clothes.*
Seal Press, 2003.

Erhardt, Virginia. *Head Over Heels: Wives Who Stay With Cross-Dressers and Transsexuals.*
Routledge, 2006.

http://www.brainyquotes.com
http://www.livingwithcrossdressing.com
http://www.tgforum.com
http://www.tinybuddha.com
http://www.plannedparenthood.org
http://www.femmefever.com
http://www.itspronouncedmetrosexual.com

Fiala, Andrew. "Toleration.",
http://www.iep.utm.edu/tolerati

Transgendered Terms

These terms come from www.itspronouncedmetrosexual.com. It is a wonderful resource for all things transgender. I strongly urge you to use it as a resource for relevant and up-to-date information.

agender – *adj.* : a person with no (or very little) connection to the traditional system of gender, no personal alignment with the concepts of either man or woman, and/or someone who sees themselves as existing without gender. Sometimes called gender neutrois, gender neutral, or genderless.

ally /"al-lie"/ – *noun* : a (typically straight and/or cisgender) person who supports and respects members of the LGBTQ community. We consider people to be active allies who take action on in support and respect.

androgyny/ous /"an-jrah-jun-ee"; "an-jrah-jun-uss"/ – *adj.* : **1** a gender expression that has elements of both masculinity and femininity.

androsexual / androphilic – *adj.* : being primarily sexually, romantically and/or emotionally attracted to some men, males, and/or masculinity.

aromantic – *adj.* : experiencing little or no romantic attraction to others and/or has a lack of interest in romantic relationships/behavior.

asexual – *adj.* : experiencing little or no sexual attraction to others and/or a lack of interest in sexual relationships/behavior.

bigender – *adj.* : a person who fluctuates between traditionally "woman" and "man" gender-based behavior and identities, identifying with both genders (and sometimes a third gender).

bicurious – *adj.* : a curiosity about having attraction to people of the same gender/sex (similar to questioning).

biological sex – *noun* : a medical term used to refer to the chromosomal, hormonal and anatomical characteristics that are used to classify an individual as female or male or intersex.

biphobia – *noun* : a range of negative attitudes (e.g., fear, anger, intolerance, invisibility, resentment, erasure, or discomfort) that one may have or express towards bisexual individuals.

bisexual – *adj.* : **1** a person who is emotionally, physically, and/or sexually attracted to males/men and females/women. **2** a person who is emotionally, physically, and/or sexually attracted to people of their gender and another gender.

butch – *noun & adj.* a person who identifies themselves as masculine, whether it be physically, mentally or emotionally.

cisgender /"siss-jendur"/ – *adj.* : a person whose gender identity and biological sex assigned at birth align (e.g., man and assigned male at birth).

cissexism – *noun* : behavior that grants preferential treatment to cisgender people, reinforces the idea that being cisgender is somehow better or more "right" than being transgender, and/or makes other genders invisible.

cisnormativity – *noun* : the assumption, in individuals or in institutions, that everyone is cisgender, and that cisgender identities are superior to trans* identities or people.

closeted – *adj.* : an individual who is not open to themselves or others about their (queer) sexuality or gender identity.

clocking – *verb.* : term used to reflect that someone transgender has been recognized as trans, usually when that person is trying to blend in with cisgender people, and not intending to be seen as anything other than the gender they present.

cross-dresser – *noun* : someone who wears clothes of another gender/sex.

deadnaming – *verb.* : the practice of uttering or publishing the name that a trans person used prior to transition.

demiromantic – *adj.* : little or no capacity to experience romantic attraction until a strong sexual or emotional connection is formed with another individual, often within a sexual relationship.

demisexual – *adj.* : little or no capacity to experience sexual attraction until a strong romantic or emotional connection is formed with another individual, often within a romantic relationship.

doxxing – *verb.* : slang for "dropping documents," a practice begun by hackers more than a decade ago. These hackers would collect and then reveal "personal and private information, including home addresses and national identity numbers.

drag king – *noun* : someone who performs masculinity theatrically.

drag queen – *noun* : someone who performs femininity theatrically.

dyke – *noun* : referring to a masculine presenting lesbian. While often used derogatorily, it can is adopted affirmatively by many lesbians (both more masculine and more feminine presenting lesbians not necessarily masculine ones) as a positive self-identity term.

fag(got) – *noun* : derogatory term referring to a gay person, or someone perceived as queer. Occasionally used as an self-identifying affirming term by some gay men, at times in the shortened form 'fag'.

feminine-of-center; masculine-of-center – *adj.* : a word that indicates a range of terms of gender identity and gender presentation for folks who present, understand themselves, and/or relate to others in a more feminine/masculine way, but don't necessarily identify as women/men.

feminine-presenting; masculine-presenting – *adj.* : a way to describe someone who expresses gender in a more feminine/masculine way.

femme – (noun & adj) someone who identifies themselves as feminine, whether it be physically, mentally or emotionally. Often used to refer to a feminine-presenting queer woman.

fluid(ity) – *adj.* : generally with another term attached, like gender-fluid or fluid-sexuality, fluid(ity) describes an identity that may change or shift over time between or within the mix of the options available (e.g., man and woman, bi and straight).

FtM / F2M; MtF / M2F – *abbreviation* : female-to-male transgender or transsexual person; male-to-female transgender or transsexual person.

gay – *adj.* : individuals who are primarily emotionally, physically, and/or sexually attracted to members of the same sex and/or gender.

gender binary – *noun* : the idea that there are only two genders and that every person is one of those two.

gender dysphoria – *noun* : the condition of feeling one's emotional and psychological identity as male or female to be opposite to one's biological sex.

gender euphoria – *noun* : The opposite of gender dysphoria. Of a cisgender person, it is a state of happiness about being male or female and having the associated gender roles and body parts.
Of a transgender person, it refers to feeling great about living as your desired gender..

gender expression – *noun* : the external display of one's gender, through a combination of dress, demeanor, social behavior, and other factors, generally made sense of on scales of masculinity and femininity.

gender fluid– *adj.* : : gender fluid is a gender identity best described as a dynamic mix of boy and girl.

gender identity – *noun* : the internal perception of an one's gender, and how they label themselves, based on how much they align or don't align with what they understand their options for gender to be.

gender non-conforming – *adj.* : **1** a gender expression descriptor that indicates a non-traditional gender presentation (masculine woman or feminine man)

gender normative / gender straight – *adj.* : someone whose gender presentation, whether by nature or by choice, aligns with society's gender-based expectations.

genderqueer – *adj.* : a gender identity label often used by people who do not identify with the binary of man/woman; or as an umbrella term for many gender non-conforming or non-binary identities (e.g., agender, bigender, genderfluid).

gender variant – *adj.* : someone who either by nature or by choice does not conform to gender-based expectations of society (e.g. transgender, transsexual, intersex, genderqueer, cross-dresser, etc).

gynesexual / gynephilic /"guy-nuh-seks-shu-uhl"/ – *adj.* : being primarily sexually, romantically and/or emotionally attracted to some woman, females, and/or femininity.

heteronormativity – *noun* : the assumption, in individuals or in institutions, that everyone is heterosexual (e.g. asking a woman if she has a boyfriend) and that heterosexuality is superior to all other sexualities.

hermaphrodite – *noun* : an outdated medical term previously used to refer to someone who was born with some combination of typically-male and typically-female sex characteristics.

heteronormativity – *noun* : the assumption, in individuals and/or in institutions, that everyone is heterosexual and that heterosexuality is superior to all other sexualities.

heterosexism – *noun* : behavior that grants preferential treatment to heterosexual people, reinforces the idea that heterosexuality is somehow better or more "right" than queerness, and/or makes other sexualities invisible.

heterosexual – *adj.* : a person primarily emotionally, physically, and/or sexually attracted to members of the opposite sex. Also known as straight.

homophobia – *noun* : an umbrella term for a range of negative attitudes (e.g., fear, anger, intolerance, resentment, erasure, or discomfort) that one may have towards members of LGBTQ community.

homosexual – *adj. & noun* : a person primarily emotionally, physically, and/or sexually attracted to members of the same sex/gender.

intersex – *adj.* : term for a combination of chromosomes, gonads, hormones, internal sex organs, and genitals that differs from the two expected patterns of male or female.

lesbian – *noun & adj.* women who have the capacity to be attracted romantically, erotically, and/or emotionally to some other women.

LGBTQ; GSM; DSG – *abbreviations* : shorthand or umbrella terms for all folks who have a non-normative (or queer) gender or sexuality, there are many different initialisms people prefer. LGBTQ is Lesbian Gay Bisexual Transgender and Queer and/or Questioning (sometimes people at a + at the end in an effort to be more inclusive); GSM is Gender and Sexual Minorities; DSG is Diverse Sexualities and Genders. Other options include the initialism GLBT or LGBT and the acronym QUILTBAG (Queer [or Questioning] Undecided Intersex Lesbian Trans* Bisexual Asexual [or Allied] and Gay [or Genderqueer]).

lipstick lesbian – *noun* : Usually refers to a lesbian with a feminine gender expression. Can be used in a positive or a derogatory way. Is sometimes also used to refer to a lesbian who is assumed to be (or passes for) straight.

metrosexual – *adj.* : a man with a strong aesthetic sense who spends more time, energy, or money on his appearance and grooming than is considered gender normative.

MSM / WSW – *abbreviations* : men who have sex with men or women who have sex with women, to distinguish sexual behaviors from sexual identities: *because a man is straight, it doesn't mean he's not having sex with men.*

Mx. / "mix" or "schwa" / – an honorific (e.g. Mr., Ms., Mrs., etc.) that is gender neutral.

outing – *verb* : involuntary or unwanted disclosure of another person's sexual orientation, gender identity, or intersex status.

pansexual – *adj.* : a person who experiences sexual, romantic, physical, and/or spiritual attraction for members of all gender identities/expressions. Often shortened to "pan."

passing – *adj. & verb* : **1** trans* people being accepted as, or able to "pass for," a member of their self-identified gender identity (regardless of sex assigned at birth) without being identified as trans*. **2** An LGB/queer individual who is believed to be or perceived as straight.

PGPs – *abbreviation* : preferred gender pronouns. Often used during introductions, becoming more common in educational institutions.

polyamory / polyamorous – *noun, adj.* refers to the practice of, desire to, or orientation towards having ethically, honest, and consensual non-monogamous relationships (i.e. relationships that may include multiple partners).

queer – *adj.* : used as an umbrella term to describe individuals who don't identify as straight. Also used to describe people who have a non-normative gender identity, or as a political affiliation.

questioning – *verb, adj.* an individual who or time when someone is unsure about or exploring their own sexual orientation or gender identity.

QPOC / QTPOC – *abbreviation* : initialisms that stand for queer people of color and queer and/or trans people of color.

same gender loving (SGL) – *adj.* : sometimes used by some members of the African-American or Black community to express an non-straight sexual orientation without relying on terms and symbols of European descent.

sex assigned at birth (SAAB) – *abbreviation* : a phrase used to intentionally recognize a person's assigned sex (not gender identity). Sometimes called "designated sex at birth" (DSAB) or "sex coercively assigned at birth" (SCAB), or specifically used as "assigned male at birth" (AMAB) or "assigned female at birth"

Living with Crossdressing: Defining a New Normal

sexual orientation – *noun* : the type of sexual, romantic, emotional/spiritual attraction one has the capacity to feel for some others, generally labeled based on the gender relationship between the person and the people they are attracted to. Often confused with sexual preference.

sexual preference – *noun* : the types of sexual intercourse, stimulation, and gratification one likes to receive and participate in. Generally when this term is used, it is being mistakenly interchanged with "sexual orientation," creating an illusion that one has a choice (or "preference") in who they are attracted to.

sex reassignment surgery (SRS) – *noun* : used by some medical professionals to refer to a group of surgical options that alter a person's biological sex.

skoliosexual – *adj.* : being primarily sexually, romantically and/or emotionally attracted to some genderqueer, transgender, transsexual, and/or non-binary people.

spiritual attraction – *noun* : a capacity that evokes the want to engage in intimate behavior based on one's experience with, interpretation of, or belief in the supernatural (e.g., religious teachings, messages from a deity), experienced in varying degrees (from little-to-none, to intense).

stealth – *adj.* : a trans person who is not "out" as trans, and is perceived by others as cisgender.

straight – *adj.* : a person primarily emotionally, physically, and/or sexually attracted to people who are not their same sex/gender. A more colloquial term for the word heterosexual.

stud – *noun* : most commonly used to indicate a Black/African-American and/or Latina masculine lesbian/queer woman. Also known as 'butch' or 'aggressive'.

TERF – *noun.* : acronym for Trans Exclusionary Radical Feminist, and is used to describe those radical feminists who oppose inclusion of transgender women in spaces they reserve exclusively for women assigned female at birth.

third gender – *noun* : for a person who does not identify with either man or woman, but identifies with another gender.

top surgery – *noun* : this term refers to surgery for the construction of a male-type chest or breast augmentation for a female-type chest.

tranny chaser – *noun.* : term describes a suitor, usually a man, whose sexual yearnings are to hook up with the object of his desire: a transsexual or transgender woman.

trans* – *adj.* : An umbrella term covering a range of identities that transgress socially defined gender norms.

transgender – *adj.* : A person who lives as a member of a gender other than that assigned at birth based on anatomical sex.

transition / transitioning – *noun, verb* this term is primarily used to refer to the process a trans* person undergoes when changing their bodily appearance either to be more congruent with the gender/sex they feel themselves to be and/or to be in harmony with their preferred gender expression.

transman; transwoman – *noun* : An identity label sometimes adopted by female-to-male transgender people or transsexuals to signify that they are men while still affirming their history as assigned female sex at birth. (sometimes referred to as transguy)

transphobia – *noun* : the fear of, discrimination against, or hatred of trans* people, the trans* community, or gender ambiguity.

transsexual – *noun and adj.* a person who identifies psychologically as a gender/sex other than the one to which they were assigned at birth.

transvestite – *noun* : a person who dresses as the binary opposite gender expression ("cross-dresses") for any one of many reasons, including relaxation, fun, and sexual gratification (often called a "cross-dresser," and should not be confused with transsexual).

triple T – *noun*. : slang for "Trannier Than Thou," an expression meant to criticize someone transgender who has either taken the position or exhibited behavior that indicates their transition was (or is) somehow better than another trans person's.

two-spirit – *noun* : is an umbrella term traditionally used by Native American people to recognize individuals who possess qualities or fulfill roles of both genders.

ze / zir / "zee", "zerr" or "zeer"/ – alternate pronouns that are gender neutral and preferred by some trans* people. They replace "he" and "she" and "his" and "hers" respectively.

About The Author

You know more about my life from reading this book than many people I interact with on a daily basis. Although I do live a dual life when it comes to colleagues, co-workers, and friends, I am an open book to the right people.

I hail from Detroit, Michigan, where the climate of acceptability in the 80s and 90s was less than stellar for crossdressers and other transgender folks. More than twenty years ago, I moved to the big city of Manhattan Island for work-related reasons and discovered a world (or a couple of boroughs) where alternative lifestyles were much more socially acceptable. Eventually, I moved out to Long Island where I have continued to live, work, love and explore both my masculinity and femininity.

I hope my journey is of value to all readers, both for the crossdresser in understanding themselves and for those partners, friends and families that need support to foster their acceptance of a person whose lifestyle may be foreign, misconstrued, and scary.

Live well, love well, and be the most beautiful creature you can be.

Made in the USA
San Bernardino, CA
23 November 2018